Designing Sorting Networks

T0183861

Sherenaz W. Al-Haj Baddar
Kenneth E. Batcher

Designing Sorting Networks

A New Paradigm

 Springer

Sherenaz W. Al-Haj Baddar
Computer Science
University of Jordan
Amman
Jordan
e-mail: s.baddar@ju.edu.jo

Kenneth E. Batcher
Emeritus Professor of Computer Science
Kent State University
Kent
USA

ISBN 978-1-4899-8990-1   ISBN 978-1-4614-1851-1 (eBook)
DOI 10.1007/978-1-4614-1851-1
Springer New York Dordrecht Heidelberg London

Cover design: Deblik

Printed on acid-free paper

Springer is part of Springer Science+Business Media (www.springer.com)

Preface

What is a Sorting Network?

It is simply a hardware sorter circuit. It consists of small switches, that we call comparators, each of which is equipped with two input lines and two output lines. The comparator receives two numbers on its input lines, compares them, and outputs the maximum on its higher output line and the minimum on its lower output line. Obviously, to carry out the sorting task, you'll need several stages (columns) of these comparators. Then, your input numbers will go through all these stages so that you receive them totally sorted on the other end of the network.

How Can You Tell if a Given Sorting Network is Better than Other Sorting Networks?

Each sorting network has two attributes that one may consider: the number of comparators used throughout all the sorting steps; and the number of sorting steps. Some researchers target designing sorting networks that use as few comparators as possible and these we refer to as efficient sorting networks. Others aim at designing sorting networks that sort using the smallest number of steps and those we refer to as fast sorting networks. Relatively speaking, if your sorting network is efficient then it does not need to be fast and the other way around.

Since it is hardware, the inter-connections between the comparators are fixed. Thus, you cannot reconfigure the comparators interconnects based on, say, the outcome of a previous comparator. This is the core difference between sorting in hardware and sorting in software. In a software sorting program, you can easily apply the decision tree model. So, based on the outcome of a comparison in step i, you decide what comparison to do in the step $i + 1$. You don't have this flexibility in hardware sorting. Thus, we say that sorting networks are oblivious. Obliviousness makes it harder for us to design an optimal sorting network.

Brief History

Many researchers were interested in designing either optimally fast or optimally efficient sorting networks since the 1950s of the past century. They experimented with small-sized sorting networks and were able to find the optimal sorting networks, in terms of efficiency, for input sizes from 1 through 8. They also found the optimal fast sorting networks, in terms of the number of steps, for input sizes 1 through 10. For the larger input sizes, it was not that easy. Nobody seemed to know how to design either optimally efficient or optimally fast sorting networks. Nobody even seemed to know for sure whether the Ω (N log$N$) boundary holds for sorting networks or not. Researchers kept coming up with designs that targeted either goal for a given input size and then conjectured that their solution is optimal. But soon afterwards, other researchers came up with even better solutions for the same input sizes. That loop kept going on until Batcher came up with the Bitonic and Odd-Even merge sorting algorithms back in 1968. These two were the first systematic algorithms for designing sorting networks no matter what input size you have. Batcher's Ω (Nlog^2N) networks are not optimal though. To prove it, Van Voorhis discovered a 16-key 9-step sorting network that is one step faster than Batcher's back in 1972. Some researchers remained interested in designing sorting networks and even applied genetic algorithms to come up with better sorting networks. The interested readers may refer to Knuth book: "The Art of Computer Programming: Volume 3 Searching and Sorting" for a comprehensive review on the history of designing sorting networks.

So, Can We Not Do Hardware Sorting in Ω (N log$N$) at All?

This question is a bit tricky!! Until the minute this book is written, the answer is yes (theoretically) and no (practically).The most significant break-through, after Batcher's two merge sorting algorithms, came 15 years later when Ajtai, Komlos, and Szemerdi introduced their optimal AKS sorting network. Unfortunately, it turned out that their sorting algorithm had a huge complexity constant that abolished the practicality of the ASK networks. Again, Batcher's merge sorting algorithms proved to be the best practical solution until this moment.

Why Bother?

Why should we bother about finding faster or more efficient sorting networks? We already have Batcher's handy algorithms for designing sorting networks, so why not just apply them and that is it?

Firstly, the question itself is interesting. You can sort in Ω (Nlog$N$) time using a software program that runs in a sequential computer. Yet you do not know how to build a hardware sorting circuit that is cost optimal. Remember, sorting in a sorting network is parallel processing in essence. If that does not sound sufficiently motivating, then consider enabling modern computer architecture. Several interesting computer architectures like Graphics Processing Units (GPUs), use Bitonic sorting or the Odd-even sorting to help them carry out their designated tasks. So, what if we discover methods for designing faster sorting networks to the benefit of these architectures? How will other computationally intensive emerging areas like Bioinformatics and Data Mining benefit from introducing faster sorting network?

In this book, we introduce different techniques for looking at the problem of designing sorting networks. We aim at sharing our experience and thoughts on designing sorting networks with the broadest range of interested audience. We hope that this will eventually help somebody discover faster, more efficient, or even a cost optimal algorithm for designing sorting networks sooner than later.

Amman   Sherenaz W. Al-Haj Baddar
Kent   Kenneth E. Batcher

Contents

Chapter 1
Early History

In the mid-1960s Goodyear Aerospace in Akron was designing parallel processors with thousands of processing elements (PE's) to perform various time-critical tasks much faster than with just a single processor. A major problem in any parallel processor is to interconnect the PE's in such a way that they can rapidly send data to each other.

One of their engineers decided to attach a destination tag to each data message and design a network of comparators to rapidly sort the messages according to these tags. Each comparator receives two messages (A and B), compares their tags, and outputs the message with the higher tag on its H output and the message with the lower tag on its L output (Fig. 1.1).

Serial sorting algorithms are much too slow so the engineer decided that a parallel sorting algorithm was needed and examined the well-known Merge-Sorting algorithm. To Merge–Sort N keys:

- first compare keys two at a time to form $N/2$ ordered lists with two keys in each list;
- then merge the $N/2$ ordered lists two at a time to form $N/4$ ordered lists with four keys in each list;
- then merge the $N/4$ ordered lists two at a time to form $N/8$ ordered lists with eight keys in each list;
- and so on; until
- two ordered lists with $N/2$ keys in each list are merged to form one ordered list containing all N keys.

The early steps of Merge-Sorting merge many short lists so one can easily speed up these steps by running their merges in parallel. But the later steps merge just a few very long lists and the usual merge algorithm runs serially so these steps will run too slow—a parallel algorithm for merging is needed.

The engineer found two parallel algorithms for merging which he called *Bitonic Merging* and *Odd–Even Merging* [1].

S. W. Al-Haj Baddar and K. E. Batcher, *Designing Sorting Networks*,   1
DOI: 10.1007/978-1-4614-1851-1_1, © Springer Science+Business Media, LLC 2011

Fig. 1.1 A comparator

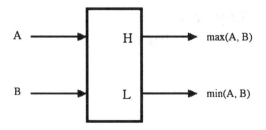

1.1 Bitonic Merging

Definition The engineer defined a *bitonic sequence* of keys to be:

1. a non-decreasing (ascending) monotonic sequence followed by a non-increasing (descending) monotonic sequence; or
2. any circular shift of a sequence that satisfies Definition 1.

As an example, Fig. 1.2 plots the graph of a 22-key bitonic sequence—the *positions* of the keys are plotted horizontally and their *values* are plotted vertically. The first 15 keys in the sequence are in non-decreasing (ascending) order and the last seven keys are in non-increasing (descending) order.

As another example, Fig. 1.3 plots the graph of a circular shift of the sequence in Fig. 1.2—each of the keys has been shifted to the right five places except the last five keys were brought around to the start.

Splitting a Bitonic Sequence: Let $A = \{a_1, a_2, \ldots, a_{2N-1}, a_{2N}\}$ be any bitonic sequence with an even number of keys, $2N$. We use a column of N comparators to compare a_i with a_{N+i} for $i = 1, 2, \ldots, N-1, N$ and then gather the N H-outputs of the comparators into an N-key sequence, H, and gather the N L-outputs of the comparators into another N-key sequence, L, as shown in Fig. 1.4.

Theorem 1.1 [1] *If $A = \{a_1, a_2, \ldots, a_{2N-1}, a_{2N}\}$ is any bitonic sequence with 2 N keys, and if*

$$H = \{\max(a_1, \ a_{N+1}), \ \max(a_2, a_{N+2}), \ldots, \ \max(a_N, a_{2N})\},$$

and if

$$L = \{\min(a_1, \ a_{N+1}), \ \min(a_2, a_{N+2}), \ldots, \ \min(a_N, a_{2N})\},$$

then:

1. *the H-sequence is a bitonic sequence of N keys;*
2. *the L-sequence is another bitonic sequence of the other N keys; and*
3. *every key in the H-sequence is greater than or equal to every key in the L-sequence (so the H-sequence contains the greatest N keys of A and the L-sequence contains the least N keys of A).*

Fig. 1.2 Graph of a 22-key
Bitonic sequence

Fig. 1.3 Graph of a circular
shift of the 22-key Bitonic
sequence

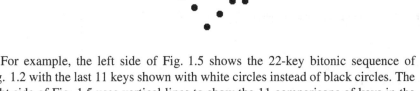

For example, the left side of Fig. 1.5 shows the 22-key bitonic sequence of Fig. 1.2 with the last 11 keys shown with white circles instead of black circles. The right side of Fig. 1.5 uses vertical lines to show the 11 comparisons of keys in the first half (black circles) with corresponding keys in the last half (white circles). Note that:

1. the *H*-sequence at the top of the comparisons is a bitonic sequence of 11 keys;
2. the *L*-sequence at the bottom of the comparisons is another bitonic sequence of 11 keys; and
3. every key in the *H*-sequence is greater than every key in the L-sequence (so the *H*-sequence contains the greatest 11 keys of the bitonic sequence of Fig. 1.2 and the L-sequence contains the least 11 keys).

As another example, Fig. 1.6 illustrates the splitting of the 22-key bitonic sequence of Fig. 1.3. Note that the *H*-sequence at the top of the comparisons is a bitonic sequence containing the greatest 11 keys of the bitonic sequence of Fig. 1.3 and the L-sequence at the bottom of the comparisons is another bitonic sequence containing the least 11 keys.

If *N* itself is an even number then another column of *N* parallel comparators can be used to further split the *H*-output sequence and the *L*-output sequence into four (*N*/2)-key bitonic sequences. If $N = 2^P$ for some integer *P* then an *N*-key bitonic sequence can be sorted into monotonic order with *P* levels of comparators where each level contains *N*/2 parallel comparators.

One can merge one ordered sequence of keys, *B*, with another ordered sequence of keys, *C*, by reversing sequence *C* and concatenating it with sequence *B* to form

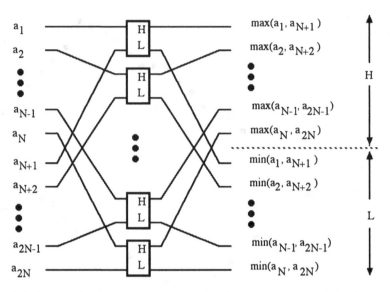

Fig. 1.4 Splitting a Bitonic sequence of 2N keys into two N-key sequences (H and L)

Fig. 1.5 Splitting the bitonic
sequence of Fig. 1.2

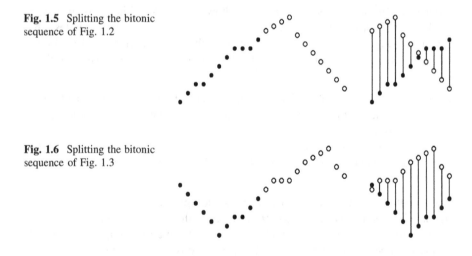

Fig. 1.6 Splitting the bitonic
sequence of Fig. 1.3

a bitonic sequence, A, of N keys which can then be ordered in $\log_2 N$ steps using $N/2$ comparators in each step.

If $N = 2^P$ for some integer P then bitonic-merge-sorting N keys can be performed in $1 + 2 + \cdots + P = P(P + 1)/2$ steps with $N/2$ parallel comparators in each step.

As an example, Fig. 1.7 illustrates bitonic-merge-sorting 8 keys in 6 steps.

Fig. 1.7 Bitonic-merge-sorting 8 keys

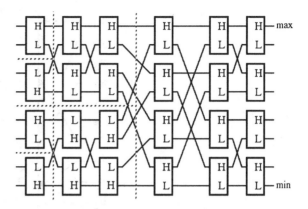

- The four comparators in the first step compare pairs of keys to form four ordered lists with 2 keys in each list. Note that the H and L outputs of two of these comparators are inverted to invert the order of their ordered lists.
- The eight comparators in Steps 2 and 3 form two ordered lists with four keys in each list. Note that the H and L outputs of the lower four comparators of these steps are inverted to invert the order of the lower list.
- The twelve comparators in Steps 4, 5, and 6 re-arrange the eight keys in the bitonic sequence from Step 3 into monotonic order to complete the sort of the 8 keys.

Remark Apparently the engineer at Goodyear Aerospace did not know his Greek from his Latin. You won't find *bitonic* in the dictionary because it mistakenly combines a Latin prefix with a Greek root—*bitonic* should really be *ditonic*.

1.2 Odd–Even Merging

It is counter-intuitive to merge two ordered lists by reversing the order of one of the lists before comparing its keys with the keys of the other list so the engineer looked for another parallel merge algorithm that eliminates the reversal—he called the following algorithm *Odd–Even Merging*.

Let $A = \{a_1, a_2, ..., a_{m-1}, a_m\}$ be a sequence of m keys in non-decreasing monotonic order:

$$a_1 \leq a_2 \leq \cdots \leq a_{m-1} \leq a_m.$$

Let $B = \{b_1, b_2, ..., b_{n-1}, b_n\}$ be a sequence of n keys in non-decreasing monotonic order:

$$b_1 \leq b_2 \leq \cdots \leq b_{n-1} \leq b_n.$$

Let $C = \{c_1, c_2, ..., c_{m+n-1}, c_{m+n}\}$ be the merge of A and B so:

$$c_1 \leq c_2 \leq \cdots \leq c_{m+n-1} \leq c_{m+n}.$$

Fig. 1.8 Odd–even merging

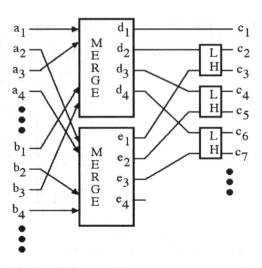

Sequence C contains some mixture of keys from A and keys from B. For example, the first 11 keys in C may be some sequence like:

$$C = \{a_1, a_2, a_3, a_4, b_1, b_2, b_3, a_5, b_4, b_5, a_6, \ldots\}$$

To maintain C in non-decreasing monotonic order, the a's and b's in this sequence may occur almost anywhere, but the subscripts of the terms follow a definite pattern. To illustrate the pattern we group the 2nd and 3rd terms of C together; the 4th and 5th terms of C together; the 6th and 7th terms of C together; the 8th and 9th terms of C together; the 10th and 11th terms of C together; etc.

$$C = \{a_1, (a_2, a_3), (a_4, b_1), (b_2, b_3), (a_5, b_4), (b_5, a_6), \ldots\}$$

Theorem 1.2 [1] *Let $A = \{a_1, a_2, \ldots, a_{m-1}, a_m\}$ be a sequence of m keys; let $B = \{b_1, b_2, \ldots, b_{n-1}, b_n\}$ be a sequence of n keys; and let $C = \{c_1, c_2, \ldots, c_{m+n-1}, c_{m+n}\}$ be the merge of A and B. Then c_1 is either a_1 or b_1 and for all positive integers i, the pair (c_{2i}, c_{2i+1}) will contain either a_j or b_j for some even integer j and either a_k or b_k for some odd integer k.*

This suggests the following parallel algorithm for merging A and B to form C (Fig. 1.8):

1. Merge the keys of A that have odd subscripts $\{a_1, a_3, a_5, a_7, \ldots\}$ with the keys of B that have odd subscripts $\{b_1, b_3, b_5, b_7, \ldots\}$ to form a sequence $D = \{d_1, d_2, d_3, d_4, \ldots\}$ of keys in non-decreasing order.
2. Merge the keys of A that have even subscripts $\{a_2, a_4, a_6, a_8, \ldots\}$ with the keys of B that have even subscripts $\{b_2, b_4, b_6, b_8, \ldots\}$ to form a sequence $E = \{e_1, e_2, e_3, e_4, \ldots\}$ of keys in non-decreasing order.

Fig. 1.9 Odd–even-merge-sorting 8 keys

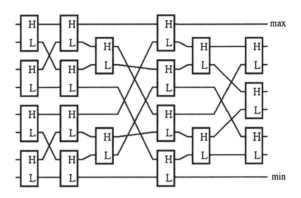

3. Then set $c_1 = d_1$ and use a column of parallel comparators to set:

$$c_{2i} = \min(d_{i+1}, \ e_i) \text{ and}$$

$$c_{2i+1} = \max(d_{i+1}, \ e_i) \quad \text{for } i = 1, 2, 3, \ldots$$

The merges in Steps 1 and 2 can be run simultaneously and each of them involves about $(m + n)/2$ keys. One can apply this same algorithm to run each of these merges in parallel. Doubling the size of a merge just adds the column of parallel comparators in Step 3 so merging m keys with n keys can be performed in $\log_2(m + n)$ steps.

If $N = 2^P$ where P is an integer then merge-sorting the N keys requires $1 + 2 + \cdots + P = P(P + 1)/2$ steps with at most $N/2$ parallel comparators in each step.

For example, Fig. 1.9 shows how 8 keys can be sorted with 19 comparators in six steps.

- the first step uses four comparators to re-arrange the 8 keys into four ordered lists with 2 keys in each list;
- the next two steps use four comparators and then two comparators to merge the four ordered lists, two at a time, into two ordered lists with 4 keys in each list; and
- the last three steps use four comparators, then two comparators, and then three comparators to merge the two ordered lists to form one ordered list containing all 8 keys.

Reference

1. Batcher KE (1968) Sorting networks and their applications. In: Proceedings of AFIPS spring joint computer conference, vol 32. AFIPS Press, Montvale, pp 307–314

Chapter 2
Software Implementations

The Goodyear Aerospace engineer was designing hardware so he described his designs with schematic diagrams like Figs. 1.8 and 1.9. But the parallel sort algorithms he found can also be implemented in *software* to be run on any parallel processor. Here we show how to implement software for the P-RAM model of a parallel processor—an EREW (Exclusive-Read Exclusive-Write) P-RAM is all that is required [1].

2.1 Software For An EREW P-RAM

A sorting algorithm in software is usually described as re-arranging an array of N keys:

K[0]	K[1]	K[2]	...	K[N-2]	K[N-1]

so that:

$$K[0] \leq K[1] \leq K[2] \leq \cdots \leq K[N-2] \leq K[N-1].$$

Each comparator in the sorting network hardware is implemented in software as a call, C(Lo, Hi), to a subroutine that compares K[Lo] with K[Hi] and swaps them if K[Lo] > K[Hi]—K is a global array of keys and index **Lo** is less than index **Hi** in each call.

The easiest way to determine the indices, **Lo** and **Hi**, in the subroutine calls is to use the sorting network hardware to sort some sequence of the N indices, {0, 1,..., N−1}, into ascending order and then to implement each hardware comparator with a call, C(L, H) where L and H are the indices on the L and H outputs of that comparator. As an example, we implement the Odd–Even-Merge-Sorting network of Fig. 1.9 in software.

1. Figure 2.1 shows how the indices flow through the network when it sorts {0, 1, 2, 3, 4, 5, 6, 7} into ascending order.

S. W. Al-Haj Baddar and K. E. Batcher, *Designing Sorting Networks*,
DOI: 10.1007/978-1-4614-1851-1_2, © Springer Science+Business Media, LLC 2011

Fig. 2.1 Odd–Even -Merge-
Sort of {0, 1, 2, 3, 4, 5, 6, 7}

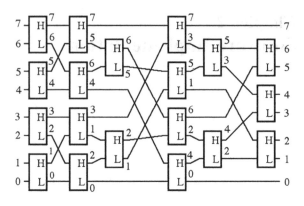

```
/* Step 1: */ C(0, 1); C(2, 3); C(4, 5); C(6, 7);
/* Step 2: */ C(0, 2); C(1, 3); C(4, 6); C(5, 7);
/* Step 3: */ C(1, 2); C(5, 6);
/* Step 4: */ C(0, 4); C(1, 5); C(2, 6); C(3, 7);
/* Step 5: */ C(2, 4); C(3, 5);
/* Step 6: */ C(1, 2); C(3, 4); C(5, 6);
```

Fig. 2.2   A program to Odd–Even -Merge-Sort 8 keys

2. Figure 2.2 shows the 19 subroutine calls in a program to sort 8 keys—the
   indices of each call are the indices that are on the L and H outputs of the
   corresponding comparator in Fig. 2.1.

In [2], software representations of sorting networks are shown with diagrams
that we call *Knuth diagrams*. Each key-index in the array being sorted is represented by a horizontal line in the Knuth diagram and each subroutine call, **C(Lo,
Hi)**, is represented by a vertical line between the horizontal lines of the **Lo** and **Hi**
indices. Figure 2.3 shows the Knuth diagram for the program in Fig. 2.2.

2.2 Re-Labeling

The program in Fig. 2.2 is not the only software implementation of the sorting
network of Fig. 1.9. For example, Fig. 2.4 shows how the indices flow through the
network when it sorts {6, 1, 4, 3, 7, 0, 2, 5} into ascending order.

Figure 2.5 shows the program created when Fig. 2.4 is used to determine the
indices of the subroutine calls.

Figure 2.6 shows the Knuth diagram for the program of Fig. 2.5.

Why are the Knuth diagrams in Figs. 2.3 and 2.6 so different?

- Step 1 of a Merge-Sort of 8 keys creates four ordered lists with two keys in each
  list. In the Knuth diagram of Fig. 2.3, these four lists are

Fig. 2.3 A Knuth diagram for Odd–Even -Merge-Sorting 8 keys

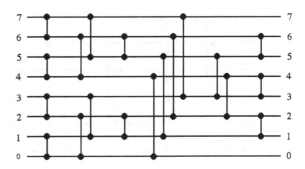

Fig. 2.4 Odd–Even -Merge-Sort of {6, 1, 4, 3, 7, 0, 2, 5}

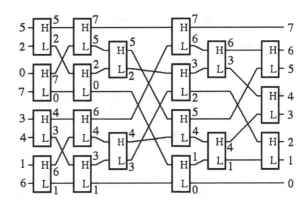

```
/* Step 1: */ C(0, 7); C(1, 6); C(2, 5); C(3, 4);
/* Step 2: */ C(0, 2); C(1, 3); C(4, 6); C(5, 7);
/* Step 3: */ C(2, 5); C(3, 4);
/* Step 4: */ C(0, 1); C(2, 3); C(4, 5); C(6, 7);
/* Step 5: */ C(1, 4); C(3, 6);
/* Step 6: */ C(1, 2); C(3, 4); C(5, 6);
```

Fig. 2.5 Another program to Odd–Even -Merge-Sort 8 keys

$$\{K[0], K[1]\}, \{K[2], K[3]\}, \{K[4], K[5]\}, \text{ and } \{K[6], K[7]\}$$

but in the Knuth diagram of Fig. 2.6, these four lists are

$$\{K[0], K[7]\}, \{K[1], K[6]\}, \{K[2], K[5]\}, \text{ and } \{K[3], K[4]\}.$$

- Steps 2 and 3 of a Merge-Sort of 8 keys merge pairs of these lists to create two ordered lists with four keys in each list. In the Knuth diagram of Fig. 2.3, these two lists are

$$\{K[0], K[1]\}, \{K[2], K[3]\} \text{ and } \{K[4], K[5]\}, \{K[6], K[7]\}$$

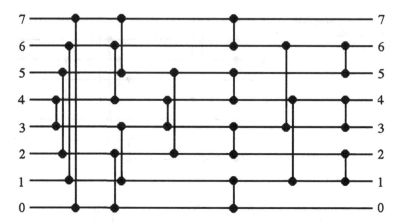

Fig. 2.6 Another Knuth diagram for Odd–Even -Merge-Sorting 8 keys

but in the Knuth diagram of Fig. 2.6, these two lists are

$$\{K[0], K[2]\}, \{K[5], K[7]\} \text{ and } \{K[1], K[3]\}, \{K[4], K[6]\}.$$

By permuting the locations of the four ordered lists created by Step 1 and permuting the locations of the two ordered lists created by Steps 2 and 3, one can create 315 different Knuth diagrams (315 different programs) to implement an 8-key Odd–Even-Merge-Sort in software.

This example illustrates how easy it is to re-label a software program or a Knuth diagram for a given sorting network to create a different program or diagram for the same network.

- Sometimes, re-labeling a software program or a Knuth diagram helps us analyze the sorting network to figure out how it works.
- Sometimes re-labeling helps us in synthesizing a new sorting network.
- Suppose somebody discovers a novel sorting network that is significantly better than previously-known networks and wants to protect the idea with a patent or a copyright - the patent or the copyright won't be worth much if it fails to cover all re-labeled versions of the network.

References

1. Akl SG (1997) Parallel computation: models and methods. Prentice-Hall, NJ
2. Knuth D (1998) The art of computer programming: volume 3 sorting and searching, 2nd edn. Addison-Wesley Longman, USA, pp 225–228

Chapter 3
Posets

When an N-key sorting network is given an unordered array of N keys:

$$\boxed{\text{K[0]}}\ \boxed{\text{K[1]}}\ \boxed{\text{K[2]}}\quad \cdots \quad \boxed{\text{K[}N\text{-2]}}\ \boxed{\text{K[}N\text{-1]}}$$

the network performs a number of comparisons and re-arrangements until the array is totally ordered so that:

$$K[0] \le K[1] \le K[2] \le \cdots \le K[N-2] \le K[N-1].$$

Each comparison, C(**Lo**, **Hi**), compares K[**Lo**] with K[**Hi**] and swaps them, if necessary, so that K[**Lo**] $\le$ K[**Hi**]. At any point in the middle of the sorting network, the array of keys is partially-ordered. Given any pair of keys, K[i] and K[j]:

- either the pair is ordered so that K[i] $\le$ K[j] or K[i] $\ge$ K[j], or
- the pair is unordered so the relation between K[i] and K[j] is not known.

A set of items where an ordering relation is established between some of the pairs of items is called a *partially-ordered set* or *poset* for short [1, 2]. The partial-ordering of the keys at any point in the sorting network can be illustrated with a *Haase diagram* [2]. Each key is denoted with an oval and for all i and j, if K[i] $\le$ K[j] then a line is drawn between their ovals with the oval for K[i] lower in the diagram than the oval for K[j].

The $\le$-relation is transitive (if $X \le Y$ and $Y \le Z$ then $X \le Z$). The clutter of lines in the Haase diagram is reduced by eliminating any line implied by transitivity. We say that Z *covers* X if $Z \ge X$ and there is no other item, Y, in the poset that is in-between Z and X; i.e., no Y where $Z \ge Y$ and $Y \ge X$. In a Haase diagram we only draw a line from Z down to X if Z *covers* X.

S. W. Al-Haj Baddar and K. E. Batcher, *Designing Sorting Networks*,
DOI: 10.1007/978-1-4614-1851-1_3, © Springer Science+Business Media, LLC 2011

3.1 Preserving Partial-Orderings

Some partial-orderings of keys established in earlier steps of a sorting network might be lost by a comparator in a later step. For example, suppose earlier steps of a sorting network have established that $A \leq B \leq C$ and that $D \leq E \leq F$ as shown on the left-side of Fig. 3.1.

The right-side of Fig. 3.1 shows the new partial-orderings if B and E are now compared to find $min(B, E)$ and $max(B, E)$. In the new ordering we have: $A \leq max(B, E)$; $D \leq max(B, E)$; $min(B, E) \leq C$; and $min(B, E) \leq F$.

The following theorem shows a way of preserving partial-orderings.

Theorem 3.1 [3] *Let A, B, C, and D be any keys. If*:

- $A \leq B$, *and*
- $C \leq D$, *and*
- *A and C are compared to find min(A, C) and max(A, C), and*
- *B and D are compared to find min(B, D) and max(B, D); then*:
- $min(A, C) \leq min(B, D)$; *and*
- $min(A, C) \leq max(A, C)$; *and*
- $min(B, D) \leq max(B, D)$; *and*
- $max(A, C) \leq max(B, D)$.

The Haase diagram of the relations in this theorem is shown in Fig. 3.2.

Theorem 3.1 can be extended to say that if corresponding keys in two similar parts of a Haase diagram are compared then the relations within each part are preserved.

3.2 An Example of Using Haase Diagrams

As an example of using Haase diagrams we consider the 8-Key Odd–Even–Merge–Sort Program in Fig. 2.2. Initially, no relations between the 8 keys are known so the Haase diagram has no lines as shown in Fig. 3.3.

Figure 3.4 shows the Haase diagram after the C(0, 1), C(2, 3), C(4, 5), and C(6, 7) comparisons in Step 1 of the program are preformed.

The C(0, 2) and C(1, 3) comparisons in Step 2 add the relations K[0] $\leq$ K[2] and K[1] $\leq$ K[3]. Since corresponding keys in the K[0] $\leq$ K[1] relation and the K[2] $\leq$ K[3] relation are compared, Theorem 3.1 applies and these two relations still hold. The C(4, 6) and C(5, 7) comparisons in Step 2 operate on the other four keys in a similar manner so Fig. 3.5 shows the Haase diagram after Step 2.

As shown in Fig. 3.6, the C(1, 2) comparison in Step 3 completes the sorting of {K[0], K[1], K[2], K[3]} into ascending order and the C(5, 6) comparison completes the sorting of {K[4], K[5], K[6], K[7]} into ascending order.

Fig. 3.1 Comparing *B* with *E* (*before* and *after*)

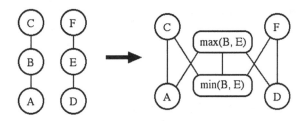

Fig. 3.2 Comparing *A* with *C* and *B* with *D* (*before* and *after*)

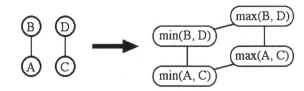

Fig. 3.3 Haase diagram before sorting

Fig. 3.4 Haase diagram after Step 1

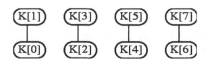

Fig. 3.5 Haase diagram after Step 2

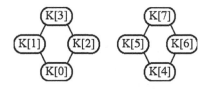

Fig. 3.6 Haase diagram after Step 3

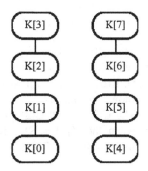

Fig. 3.7 Haase diagram after
Step 4

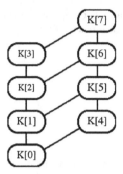

Fig. 3.8 Haase diagram after
Step 5

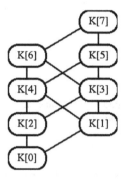

Fig. 3.9 Haase diagram after
Step 6

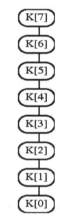

The C(0, 4), C(1, 5), C(2, 6), and C(3, 7) comparisons in Step 4 compare corresponding keys between the {K[0], K[1], K[2], K[3]} chain and the {K[4], K[5], K[6], K[7]} chain so Theorem 3.1 applies and the two chains are preserved as shown in Fig. 3.7.

The C(2, 4) and C(3, 5) comparisons of Step 5 compare corresponding keys between the K[2] ≤ K[3] relation and the K[4] ≤ K[5] relation so these two relations still hold. The Haase diagram showing the relations after Step 5 can be drawn several different ways—Fig. 3.8 shows the diagram with the even-indexed keys on the left and the odd-indexed keys on the right to emphasize the fact that the program is performing an Odd–Even–Merge–Sort.

The C(1, 2), C(3, 4), and C(5, 6) comparisons in Step 6 complete the sort by comparing odd-indexed keys with even-indexed keys. The Haase diagram in Fig. 3.9 now shows all eight keys in an ordered chain.

A poset with a Haase diagram that consists of one connected component (like Fig. 3.9) is called a **single-segment poset**. Alternatively, if the Haase diagram depicts two or more disconnected components (like Fig. 3.4), then we call such a poset a **multi-segment poset**.

Remark In some reference books, *Haase* is spelled *Hasse*.

References

1. Birkhoff G (1967) Lattice theory. American Mathematical Society, vol 25, 3rd edn. Colloquium Publications, Providence, pp 1–20
2. Rosen K (2003) Discrete mathematics and its applications, 5th edn. McGraw-Hill, New York, pp 231–245
3. Al-Haj Baddar S, Batcher KE (2009) Finding faster sorting networks using Sortnet. VDM Publishing, Saarbrücken, pp 4–17

Chapter 4
The 0/1-Principle

How can we show that a given series of comparators is really a sorting network for N keys? One way is to show that the series of comparators sorts all $N!$ permutations of N distinct keys but the 0/1-Principle says that we need only consider the 2^N cases where each key is either a 0 or a 1.

0/1-Principle [1, 2]: If a series of comparators sorts all 2^N sequences of N zeroes and ones then it will also sort any sequence of N arbitrary keys.

The 0/1-Principle can be proven by showing that if a series of comparators fails to sort some sequence of N arbitrary keys then there exists a sequence of N zeroes and ones that the series of comparators will also fail to sort.

Definition We say that a sequence of N keys is a *0/1-case* if each of its keys has either a 0-value or a 1-value.

Let 0/1-case A have exactly j 0-values and $(N - j)$ 1-values. Each comparator in a sequence of comparators either swaps the values in a pair of keys or not, so case A still has exactly j 0-values and $(N - j)$ 1-values after any series of comparators. The series of comparators sorts case A if and only if it re-arranges its keys so that all j 0-values are in K[0] through K[$j - 1$] and all $(N - j)$ 1-values are in K[j] through K[$N - 1$].

K[0]	K[1]	..	K[j-2]	K[j-1]	K[j]	K[j+1]	..	K[N-2]	K[N-1]
0	0	..	0	0	1	1	..	1	1

The number of 0-values in a 0/1-case can be anywhere from 0 through N so there are exactly $(N + 1)$ sorted 0/1-cases of N keys. A series of comparators sorts all 0/1-cases if and only if it reduces the number of 0/1-cases from 2^N down to $N + 1$.

S. W. Al-Haj Baddar and K. E. Batcher, *Designing Sorting Networks*,
DOI: 10.1007/978-1-4614-1851-1_4, © Springer Science+Business Media, LLC 2011

4.1 A Partial-Order Relation Between 0/1-Cases

A very useful partial-order relation can be defined between 0/1-cases. We denote this relation with $\ll$ instead of $\leq$ to emphasize the fact that it is a relation between 0/1-cases and not between keys.

Definition If $A = \{K[0], K[1],\ldots, K[N-1]\}$ and $A' = \{K'[0], K'[1],\ldots, K'[N-1]\}$ are two 0/1-cases then we say that $A \ll A'$ if and only if there is no index m where $K[m] = 1$ and $K'[m] = 0$.

The $\ll$ relation is preserved by comparison operations as illustrated by Theorem 4.1 [3].

Theorem 4.1 Let A and A' be any two 0/1-cases with the same number of keys and let C(Lo, Hi) be a comparison between any two of the keys, Lo and Hi. If $A \ll A'$ before the C(Lo, Hi) operation is applied to A and A', then $A \ll A'$ after the C(Lo, Hi) operation is applied to A and A' [1].

Since a sorting network is just a series of comparator operations, the $\ll$ relation is preserved throughout all steps in the network.

4.2 An Example

As an example we consider the sixteen 0/1-cases of the 4-key sorting network shown in Fig. 4.1.

The Haase diagram of the 16 unsorted 0/1-cases of 4 keys is shown in Fig. 4.2. Note that the 16 cases are distributed across the five levels in this diagram according to how many 0-keys they have:

- the highest level has the single case with no 0-keys;
- the four cases on the next lower level each have one 0-key;
- the six cases on the next lower level each have two 0-keys;
- the four cases on the next lower level each have three 0-keys; and
- the lowest level has the single case with four 0-keys.

Step 1: Comparisons C(0,1) and C(2,3) change seven of the 16 cases so they coalesce with other cases–after step 1 there are only nine distinct cases to consider as shown in Fig. 4.3

Step 2: Comparisons C(0,2) and C(1,3) in step 2 change three of the nine cases so they coalesce with other cases–after step 2 there are only six distinct cases to consider as shown in Fig. 4.4

Step 3: Operator C(1,2) in step 3 changes case 0101 so it coalesces with case 0011—after step 3 there are only five distinct cases which are totally ordered in a chain as shown in Fig. 4.5

Fig. 4.1 An odd–even–merge–sort of 4 keys

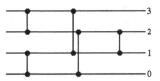

Fig. 4.2 The 16 unsorted 0/1-cases of 4 keys [3]

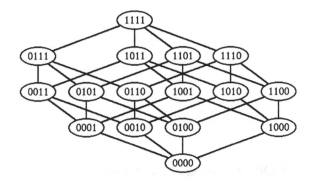

Fig. 4.3 The remaining nine cases after treatment by C(0, 1) and C(2, 3) [3]

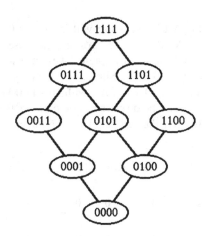

Fig. 4.4 The remaining six cases after treatment by C(0, 2) and C(1, 3) [3]

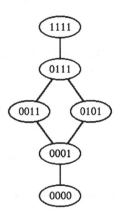

Fig. 4.5 The remaining five
cases after treatment by
C(1, 2) [3]

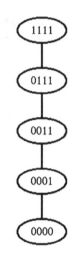

4.3 Odd-Cases and Even-Cases

Let A be a 0/1-case with exactly j 0-keys. We ignore the cases where $j = 0$ and $j = N$ because the keys of these cases are already sorted.

Changing any single 1-key of A to a 0-key produces another 0/1-case, A', with $(j + 1)$ 0-keys. Similarly, changing any single 0-key of A to a 1-key produces another 0/1-case, A'', with $(j - 1)$ 0-keys. Note that $A' \ll A \ll A''$.

Let S be a series of comparators that sorts A' and A'' into non-decreasing order so after the last step of A we have:

Case	K[0]	K[1]	..	K[j-2]	K[j-1]	K[j]	K[j+1]	..	K[N-2]	K[N-1]
A''	0	0	..	0	1	1	1	..	1	1
A'	0	0	..	0	0	0	1	..	1	1

But $A' \ll A \ll A''$ and these relations are preserved throughout series S so at the end of S, case A can only be in one of two states:

Case	State	K[0]	K[1]	...	K[j-2]	K[j-1]	K[j]	K[j+1]	...	K[N-2]	K[N-1]
A	1	0	0	...	0	0	1	1	...	1	1
	2	0	0	...	0	1	0	1	...	1	1

Adding comparator $C(j - 1, j)$ after series S will sort case A.

We say that a 0/1-case is an *odd case* if it has an odd number of 0-keys or an *even case* if it has an even number of 0-keys.

If S is a series of comparators that sorts all odd cases of N keys, then adding a single step containing comparators $C(1,2)$, $C(3,4)$, $C(5,6)$,..., after series S will sort all even cases to complete the sort of the N keys; or

If S is a series of comparators that sorts all even cases of N keys, then adding a single step comparators $C(0,1)$, $C(2,3)$, $C(4,5)$,..., after series S will sort all odd cases to also complete the sort of the N keys.

To design an N-key sorting network one doesn't have to consider all 2^N 0/1-cases–just the 2^{N-1} odd cases (or the 2^{N-1} even cases.) Once these cases are sorted, the addition of a single step of comparators will sort all the other cases.

4.4 Bracket Cases

Let $0 < i < k < N$ and assume that a series of comparators has sorted all 0/1-cases with i zeroes and all 0/1-cases with k zeroes. Let A be any 0/1-case with j zeroes where $i < j < k$. At the end of this series of comparators we have:

(Sorted case with k zeroes) $\ll$ (Case A) $\ll$ (Sorted case with i zeroes)

So at the end of this series of comparators we have: (Table 4.1).

where each key of case A with a ?-mark may have a 0-value or a 1-value. To sort all cases with j zeroes (where $i < j < k$) it is only necessary to sort the keys in $\{K[i], K[i+1],..., K[k-1]\}$

We say that 0/1-cases with i zeroes and 0/1-cases with k zeroes are *bracket cases* [1] because sorting all these cases brackets the unsorted keys of all intermediate 0/1-cases to $\{K[i], K[i+1],..., K[k-1]\}$.

4.5 0/1-Case Analysis Versus POSET Analysis

To analyze what is happening in the midst of a series of comparators one can examine the Haase diagram of the poset as described in Chap. 3 and/or examine the 0/1-cases as described in this chapter. An un-ordered set of N keys has 2^N 0/1-cases so examining the 0/1-cases is much harder than examining the poset relations between the keys so why should we consider the 0/1-cases at all? Three reasons are:

1. The 0/1-case analysis can be simplified by only examining the odd cases, the even cases, or certain bracket cases.
2. Sometimes poset analysis of the keys doesn't give us a complete picture of what's happening. For example, it doesn't give us the complete picture of Bitonic merging.

Table 4.1 Bracketing case A

	K[0]	K[1]	:	K[i − 2]	K[i − 1]	K[i]	K[i + 1]	:	K[k − 2]	K[k − 1]	K[k]	K[k + 1]	...	K[N − 2]	K[N − 1]
Sorted case with i zeroes	0	0	:	0	0	1	1	:	1	1	1	1	...	1	1
Case A	0	0	:	0	0	?	?	:	?	?	1	1	...	1	1
Sorted case with k zeroes	0	0	:	0	0	0	0	:	0	0	1	1	...	1	1

3. The 0/1-case analysis of a sorting network can be automated with a software program like Sortnet.

References

1. Knuth D (1998) The art of computer programming volume 3 sorting and searching, 2nd edn. Addison-Wesley Longman, New York, pp 225–228
2. Cormen T, Leiserson C, Rivest R, Stein C (2001) Introduction to algorithms, 2nd edn. McGraw-Hill Book Company, New York
3. Al-Haj Baddar S, Batcher KE (2009) Finding faster sorting networks using Sortnet. VDM Publishing House Ltd., Saarbrücken

Chapter 5
A 16-Key Sorting Network

Figure 51 in [1] shows a 16-key sorting network that was discovered by David C. Van Voorhis. We analyze his network here because it is faster than the merge-sorting networks for 16 keys (9 steps instead of 10 steps).

The Knuth diagram of the first four steps of the network is shown in Fig. 5.1 and the Knuth diagram of the last five steps is shown in Fig. 5.2.

5.1 The First Four Steps of the Network

Figure 5.3 shows the Haase diagram after the first four steps of the network. It shows that these steps put the minimum key into K[0], the maximum key into K[15], and the other 14 keys into three sets: {K[7], K[11], K[13], K[14]}, {K[3], K[5], K[6], K[9], K[10], K[12]}, and {K[1], K[2], K[4], K[8]}, with some partial-orderings between the keys in different sets. In Lattice Theory, this partial-ordering of the 16 keys is called a *complemented distributive lattice* or a *Boolean Algebra Boolean Algebra* [2].

5.2 Re-Labeling the Network

A more logical placement of the 14 keys in the three sets between K[0] and K[15] would be to put:

- K[11] through K[14] in the top set,
- K[5] through K[10] in the middle set, and
- K[1] through K[4] in the bottom set.

We re-label the network by exchanging K[3] with K[8] and by exchanging K[7] with K[12] as shown in Fig. 5.4.

S. W. Al-Haj Baddar and K. E. Batcher, *Designing Sorting Networks*,
DOI: 10.1007/978-1-4614-1851-1_5, © Springer Science+Business Media, LLC 2011

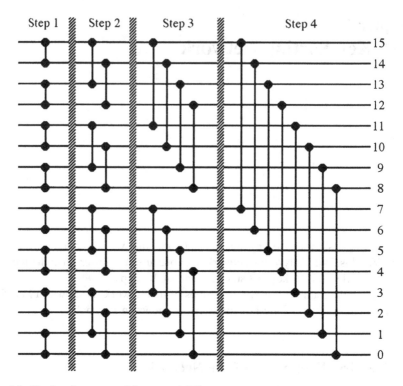

Fig. 5.1 The first four steps of the network [1]

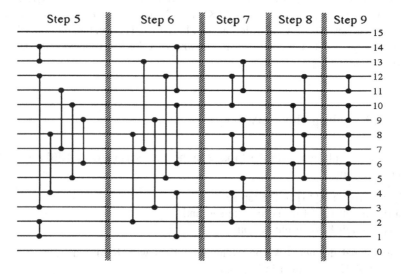

Fig. 5.2 The last five steps of the network [1]

Fig. 5.3 The Haase diagram
after the first four steps [3]

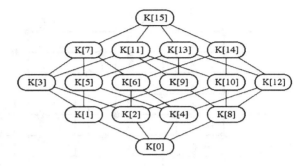

Fig. 5.4 The Haase diagram
after the first four steps
(re-labeled)

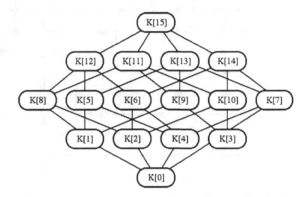

Re-Labeling the Knuth Diagram: As described in Sect. 2.2, first we see how the network re-arranges {0, 1, 2, 8, 4, 5, 6, 12, 3, 9, 10, 11, 7, 13, 14, 15} into ascending order (Figs. 5.5 and 5.6).

Then we draw the Knuth diagram for the re-labeled network (Figs. 5.7 and 5.8).

5.3 The Last Five Steps of the Network

Boxes *A*, *B*, *C*, and *D* in Fig. 5.8 illustrate the fact that the last five steps of the network contain four copies of a 4-key sorting network:

- Box *A* sorts K[11] through K[14] into ascending order.
- Box *D* sorts K[1] through K[4] into ascending order.
- Box *B* combines K[11] (the minimum of K[11] through K[14]) with K[8] through K[10] and sorts the four keys into ascending order.
- Box *C* combines K[4] (the maximum of K[1] through K[4]) with K[5] through K[7] and sorts the four keys into ascending order.

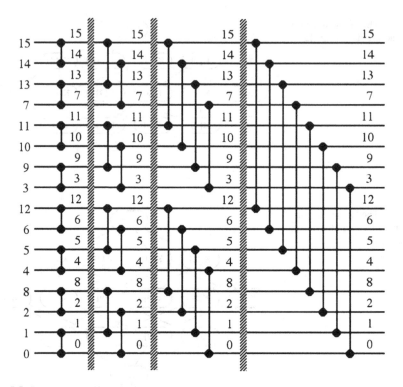

Fig. 5.5 Re-arranging {0, 1, 2, 8, 4, 5, 6, 12, 3, 9, 10, 11, 7, 13, 14, 15} into ascending order (first four steps)

Steps 5 and 6 also contain six comparators comparing keys in the middle set of keys, {K[5], K[6], K[7], K[8], K[9], K[10]}, to partially order the {K[5], K[6], K[7]} sub-set below the {K[8], K[9], K[10]} sub-set.

Step 9 contains five comparators to finish sorting certain even cases (0/1-cases with 4, 6, 8, 10, or 12 zeroes.) Steps 1 through 8 of the network has to sort all odd cases and all 0/1-cases with 2 or 14 zeroes.

Figure 5.9 shows the Haase diagram after Step 6 considering only the odd 0/1-cases (adding the 0/1-cases with 2 or 14 zeroes does not change the diagram). For these 0/1-cases the first six steps partition the 16 keys into four groups with every key in each group less than or equal to every key in the next higher group:

{K[0], K[1], K[2], K[3]} ≤ {K[4], K[5], K[6], K[7]} ≤ {K[8], K[9], K[10], K[11]} ≤ {K[12], K[13], K[14], K[15]}.

The first six steps also start sorting the keys in {K[11], K[12], K[13], K[14]} and the keys in {K[1], K[2], K[3], K[4]} so K[11] can be grouped with {K[8], K[9], K[10]} and K[4] can be grouped with {K[5], K[6], K[7]}.

15	15	15	15	15	15
14	14	14	14	14	14
13	13	13	13	13	13
7	8	8	10	11	12
11	12	12	12	12	11
10	10	10	8	9	10
9	9	9	11	10	9
3	4	4	6	7	8
12	11	11	9	8	7
6	6	6	4	5	6
5	5	5	7	6	5
4	3	3	3	3	4
8	7	7	5	4	3
2	2	2	2	2	2
1	1	1	1	1	1
0	0	0	0	0	0

Fig. 5.6 Re-arranging {0, 1, 2, 8, 4, 5, 6, 12, 3, 9, 10, 11, 7, 13, 14, 15} into ascending order (last five steps)

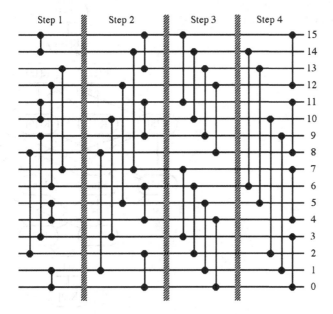

Fig. 5.7 The first four steps re-labeled

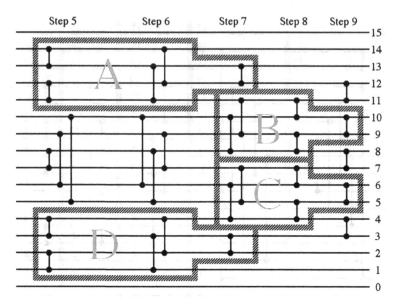

Fig. 5.8 The last five steps re-labeled

Fig. 5.9 Haase diagram after
step six for only the odd
0/1-cases

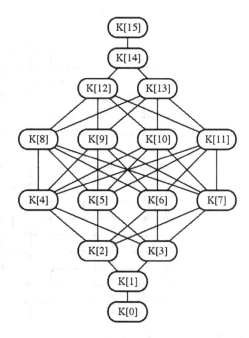

5.4 Summary of Analysis

The 16-key sorting network discovered by David C. Van Voorhis uses the common divide-and-conquer strategy of algorithms:

- The first six steps partition the keys into four 4-key groups (at least for the odd 0/1-cases) with every key in each group less than or equal to every key in the next higher group—this reduces the problem to sorting the keys within each group.
- Steps 5–8 sort the keys within each group (at least for the odd 0/1-cases).
- Step 9 finishes sorting all the even 0/1-cases to complete the sort of all 16 keys.

References

1. Knuth D (1998) The art of computer programming: sorting and searching, vol 3, 2nd edn. Addison-Wesley Longman, Boston, pp 225–228
2. Birkhoff G (1967) Lattice theory. American Mathematical Society, vol 25, 3rd edn. Colloquium Publications, Providence
3. Al-Haj Baddar S, Batcher KE (2009) Finding faster sorting networks using Sortnet. VDM Publishing, Saarbrücken

Chapter 6
The Sortnet Program

The Sortnet program is a useful tool for analyzing and/or synthesizing an N-key sorting network where $N \leq 32$ [1]. A Comparator List (CL) is an ordered list of comparators and Sortnet commands create, manage, and save CLs. After creating a CL, other Sortnet commands can be used to: create the set of 0/1-cases that corresponds to the CL list; count these cases; display the corresponding poset of the keys; display the poset of the keys after selecting particular cases; change the comparators in the CL to relabel the keys in the poset; and display the corresponding Shmoo chart considering all or a selected set of the 0/1-cases.

6.1 The Sortnet Commands

sortnet-> indicates that Sortnet is waiting to receive a user command.

A Sortnet command contains: a mnemonic that describes the operation to be performed; a list of zero or more parameters; and a semi-colon (;), if necessary, to indicate the end of the parameter list. Whitespace (one or more spaces, tabs, or newlines) are used to separate the mnemonic from the first parameter, each parameter from the next, and the last parameter from the semi-colon (;) at the end of the parameter list [1, 2]. Obviously, each command should be followed by a newline (return-key) to make sure that the OS sends it to Sortnet.

A Sortnet mnemonic has one, two, or three components separated by "."(dots). The first component describes an action, the second component (if exists) describes the object on which the action will be performed, and the third component (if exists) is a modifier.

The following commands are useful for creating and modifying the CL [1, 2]:

- **ENT.CE numlo numhi ... numlo numhi;**
  Enter comparators from the keyboard into the CL. The first two integers specify the **Lo** (**low**) and **Hi** (**high**) indices of the first comparator, the next two integers specify the **Lo** and **Hi** indices of the second comparator, etc. For example,

S. W. Al-Haj Baddar and K. E. Batcher, *Designing Sorting Networks*,
DOI: 10.1007/978-1-4614-1851-1_6, © Springer Science+Business Media, LLC 2011

Fig. 6.1 The SHOW.CE
display of the five
comparators of Fig. 4.1

```
/* STEP 1 */

    0  1    2  3

/* STEP 2 */

    0  2    1  3

/* STEP 3 */

    1  2

/* 5 comparators in 3 steps. */
```

ENT.CE 0 1 2 3 0 2 1 3 1 2; will enter the five comparators of Fig. 4.1 into the CL.

- **SHOW.CE**
  Display the comparators in the CL on the monitor with comments to indicate the step to which the listed comparators belong. For example, Fig. 6.1 shows the display if the CL contains the five comparators of Fig. 4.1.
- **WR.CE filename**
  Write the comparators in the CL into the file called **filename**.
- **RD.CE filename**
  Read comparators into the CL from the file **filename**. The file can be created by **WR.CE** and in that case Sortnet neglects the comments in the file.
- **CUT.CE.STEPS numlaststep**
  Delete all the comparators in the CL that exist in steps after **numlaststep**. See Sect. 6.4 for an example of how a **CUT.CE.STEPS** command can be used to help relabel a sorting network.
- **CUT.CE.KEYS numlo numhi**
  Remove all comparators in the CL using keys with indices less than **numlo** and/ or keys with indices greater than **numhi**. Then subtract **numlo** from the **Lo** and **Hi** indices of every remaining comparator.
  Note that this command can be used to reduce an N-key sorting network to an M-key sorting network where $M < N$. If the original CL sorts the keys in locations 0 through $N-1$ into ascending order and if **numhi** $< N$, then the new CL is a (**numhi** − **numlo** + 1)-key sorting network that sorts the keys in locations 0 through **numhi** − **numlo** into ascending order.
- **REL.CE**
  Relabel the comparators in the CL to relabel the keys as ordered by the current poset. See Sect. 6.4 for an example of using a **REL.CE** command to relabel a sorting network.
- **CLR.CE**
  Removes all comparators in the current CL.

Fig. 6.2 The SHOW.POSET
display for the poset in
Fig. 3.5

```
POSET CONSIDERING ALL 0/1-CASES
+-----+----------------+----------+---------+
|     | Number of Keys |   Keys   |   Keys  |
|  k  +-------+--------+ covering | covered |
|     |  > k  |  < k   |    k     |  by k   |
+-----+-------+--------+----------+---------+
|  0  |   3   |   0    |  1   2   |         |
|  1  |   1   |   1    |  3       |  0      |
|  2  |   1   |   1    |  3       |  0      |
|  3  |   0   |   3    |          |  1   2  |
+-----+-------+--------+----------+---------+
|  4  |   3   |   0    |  5   6   |         |
|  5  |   1   |   1    |  7       |  4      |
|  6  |   1   |   1    |  7       |  4      |
|  7  |   0   |   3    |          |  5   6  |
+-----+-------+--------+----------+---------+
```

Other Sortnet commands are as follows:

- **GEN.CASES**
  Creates a set of 0/1-cases using the current CL.
- **SHOW.POSET**
  Display a 5-column table illustrating the poset of the keys created by the current
  set of 0/1-cases. Each key has a row in this table such that:

  - column 1 designates the index of the key, K[k];
  - column 2 designates the number of keys that are greater than K[k];
  - column 3 designates the number of keys that are less than K[k];
  - column 4 designates the indices of keys that cover K[k] (refer to chapter); and
  - column 5 designates the indices of keys that are covered by K[k] (refer
    to Chap. 3).

  A horizontal line separates the segments constituting the poset. Also, the keys
  in each segment are ordered according to the number of keys greater than them. As
  an example, Fig. 6.2 shows the table for the poset diagrammed in Fig. 3.5.

- **WR.POSET filename**
  Write to the indicated file, a 5-column table describing the poset of the keys
  created by the current set of 0/1-cases. The contents of the file are the same as
  the **SHOW.POSET** display.
- **SHOW.CASECNTS**
  Display on the monitor the number of 0/1-cases that have exactly z zeroes for all
  z in the range 0–N where N is the number of keys to be sorted.
- **SEL.CASES num$_1$ num$_2$ ... num$_m$;**
  Define a subset of the set of 0/1-cases. This subset contains all 0/1-cases with
  exactly **num** zeroes for all the **num$_i$** values in the parameter list.
- **SHOW.SHMOO**
  This command displays a chart which is an N-row $\times$ $N + 1$ -column matrix. If
  "class Z_j" denotes the set of all 0/1-cases with exactly j zeros in a given N-key
  sorting network, then each class Z_j has a column and each key has row in the

Fig. 6.3 The
SHOW.SHMOO display for
the poset in Fig. 3.5

```
sortnet -> SHOW.SHMOO


   Number of Zeroes in Case
   000000000    No. of Cases        No. of Dashes
   876543210    where key = 1

7: 011111111 :          19                   0
6: 00---1111 :          14                   3
5: 00---1111 :          14                   3
3: 00---1111 :          14                   3
4: 0000---11 :           6                   3
2: 0000---11 :           6                   3
1: 0000---11 :           6                   3
0: 000000001 :           1                   0
```

Fig. 6.4 The
SHOW.GOODCE display for
the poset in Fig. 3.5

```
sortnet -> SHOW.GOODCE

Number of Shmoo Chart Dashes Removed by Each Possible CE
for all cases.

High:  7  6  5  4  3  2  1
  Low
   0:   .  .  .  .  .  .  .
   1:   .  2  .  3  .  3
   2:   .  .  2  3  .
   3:   .  3  3  2
   4:   .  .  .
   5:   .  3
   6:   .
```

Shmoo chart. Figure 6.3 illustrates the Shmoo chart that corresponds to the poset depicted in Fig. 3.5.

The columns in the chart are ordered with class Z_N at the left of the chart and class Z_0 at the right of it. The entry in row i and column j is [1]:

- 1: if key at location i, in every case in class Z_j, equals one;
- 0: if key at location i, in every case in class Z_j, equals zero; or
- -: if there is at least one case in class Z_j, where key at location i equals zero and at least one case where it equals one in the same class.

The keys in the Shmoo chart are ordered based on the number of 0/1-cases in which the key is equal to one. If two or more keys have the same number of cases in which their value is one, then they are ordered by their indices in decreasing order. After totally sorting all the keys in a network, the Shmoo chart becomes dash-free.

- **SHOW.GOODCE**
  Display the number of dashed removed by each possible comparator in the form of an upper triangular $(N-1) \times (N-1)$ table, where N is the number of keys. If a given comparator does not eliminate any dashes, then a dot is displayed. Figure 6.4 illustrates the output of the **SHOW.GOODCE** command after generating the cases of the poset depicted in Fig. 3.5.

Fig. 6.5 The SHOW.DIFF
display for the poset in
Fig. 3.5

```
sortnet-> SHOW.DIFF

Number of 0/1-Cases Affected by each Possible CE for all cases.

Maximum Value = 3

High:  7  6  5  4  3  2  1
 Low
   0:  0  0  0  0  0  0  0
   1:  0  1  0  3  0  3
   2:  0  0  1  3  0
   3:  0  3  3  1
   4:  0  0  0
   5:  0  3
   6:  0|
```

Fig. 6.6 The
SHOW.BESTCE display for
the poset in Fig. 3.5

```
sortnet-> SHOW.BESTCE

Best Comparators considering all cases.

Step Dashes CasesSwapped    Comparators

  4      3              3    1:2 1:4 2:4 3:5 3:6 5:6
```

- **SHOW.DIFF**
  Display the number of 0/1-cases that get altered by each comparator. The output of this command is displayed in the form of an upper triangular $(N - 1) \times (N - 1)$ table. A zero is displayed if such a comparison modifies no 0/1-cases. The output of the **SHOW.DIFF** command when applied to the 0/1-cases resulting from the poset in Fig. 3.5 is illustrated in Fig. 6.5.

- **SHOW.BESTCE**
  Displays the CEs that remove the most dashes and/or modify the most cases together with the earliest step in which they can be used. The network designer selects the CEs they believe are the best and adds them to the CL. Figure 6.6 depicts the **BESTCE** output obtained after generating the 0/1-cases of the poset described in Fig. 3.5.

- **SHOW.POSET.SEL**
  Display on the monitor, a 5-column table like that of **SHOW.POSET** except that the poset considers only those 0/1-cases that are in the subset that was defined by **SEL.CASES**.

- **WR.POSET.SEL filename**
  Write to the indicated file, a 5-column table describing the poset of the keys created by the subset defined by **SEL.CASES**. The contents of the file are the same as the **SHOW.POSET.SEL** display.

- **SHOW.MENU**
  Display the menu of commands on the monitor.

- **QUIT**
  Exit the Sortnet program.

6.2 Customizing Sortnet

Some users may find it difficult to enter the characters of the command mnemonics. So, a user can customize his/her own copy of Sortnet by creating a text file, **EQUIV.LST**, defining a set of equivalent mnemonics that he/she can easily enter.

Each equivalence in **EQUIV.LST** is defined by: **newmnemonic = oldmnemonic;** where **newmnemonic** is the new mnemonic being defined and **oldmnemonic** is a previously-defined mnemonic which **newmnemonic** will be equivalent to. For example, adding:

$$\text{haase} = \textbf{SHOW.POSET};$$

to **EQUIV.LST** allows the user to enter **haase** instead of **SHOW.POSET** as a command to display the description of a poset on the monitor.

EQUIV.LST should be in the same directory as Sortnet and it is read by Sortnet before it prompts for the first command.

6.3 How Sortnet Works

Sortnet is written in the C language. Here we explain how some parts of the Sortnet program function.

Each 0/1-case
Assume that you are designing an N-key sorting network. Sortnet keeps a set of 0/1-cases and each one of these cases is a sequence of N bits with each bit showing the value, **0** or **1**, of one of the keys for that case. It is suitable to limit N to 32, due to the fact that the length of an integer in C is 32 bits.

The Number of 0/1-cases
The N keys are not sorted at all before applying the network comparators. Thus, the program is supposed to begin with 2^N 0/1-cases. If $N = 32$ then $2^N = 2^{32} = 4{,}294{,}967{,}296$. Does Sortnet really start with that many 0/1-cases? No. If the poset has two or more segments, Sortnet only has to maintain the 0/1-cases for each segment in a separate linked-list.

The poset has N segments, at the very beginning, with each segment containing just one key. Thus, there are only two 0/1-cases for that segment: a case with one 0 and a case with one 1. Consequently, Sortnet begins with N linked-lists where each list has only two cases.

Treating Each Comparator
The comparators in the CL are handled one at a time. The comparator C(**Lo**, **Hi**) is handled by checking whether or not **Lo** and **Hi** are in the same segment of the poset:

- If **Lo** and **Hi** belong to the same segment of the poset, then Sortnet checks all the 0/1-cases for that segment. If it finds a case where **Lo** = 1 and **Hi** = 0, then it swaps the two values.
- If **Lo** and **Hi** belong to two different segments of the poset, then Sortnet uses a nested loop to concatenate every 0/1-case of one segment with every 0/1-case of the other segment. Afterwards, Sortnet checks to see if there is a combination where **Lo** = 1 and **Hi** = 0. If that is the case, then it swaps the two values. The two segments are now combined into one segment in which both **Lo** and **Hi** appear.

Eliminating Duplicate Cases
Generating duplicate cases is possible but it is not acceptable to store them. Thus, Sortnet uses hashing to eliminate duplicate cases. The new cases generated when a comparator is handled are temporarily stored in P separate linked-lists where P is a prime number. Let C denote a generated case, then it will be stored in the linked-list C mod P only if it does not already exist in the designated linked-list.

Keeping Track of Keys in Each Segment
To keep track of which keys are in each segment, Sortnet uses the *Make-Set*, *Union*, and *Find-Set* operations described in Chap. 21 of the Second Edition of *Introduction to Algorithms* by Cormen, Leiserson, Rivest, and Stein [3].

Example—BOOL(16)
To illustrate how Sortnet reduces the number of cases it handles we use the CL that forms BOOL (16). The CL of this BOOL is depicted in Fig. 5.1.

- Initially each key is in a separate segment so there are only 32 cases instead of 2^{16} cases.
- The 8 comparators in Step 1 form 8 segments with three cases in each segment; 24 cases instead of 3^8 cases.
- The 8 comparators in Step 2 form 4 segments with six cases in each segment; 24 cases instead of 6^4 cases.
- The 8 comparators in Step 3 form 2 segments with twenty cases in each segment; 40 cases instead of 20^2 cases.
- The 8 comparators in Step 4 form a one-segment poset with 168 cases.

6.4   Example: Relabeling the Sorting Network of Chapter 5

Chapter 5 describes an analysis of a 16-key sorting network that uses 9 steps. In this analysis the comparators in all nine steps of the network were relabeled according to the Haase diagram of the first four steps. Here we describe how the commands of Sortnet can be used to perform this relabeling:

1. Use **ENT.CE** commands to build a CL containing all 61 comparators of the network.

2. Use a **WR.CE** command to save the CL in a file.
3. Use a **CUT.CE.STEPS 4** command to remove all comparators in steps 5 through 9 of the network.
4. Use a **GEN.CASES** command to generate the set of 0/1-cases from the first four steps of the network.
5. Use a **SHOW.POSET** command to get a description of the poset created by this set of 0/1-cases. The 5-column table displayed should correspond to the Haase diagram in Fig. 3.5.
6. Use a **CLR.CE** command to clear out all comparators in the CL.
7. Use a **RD.CE** command to restore the CL to that saved in step 2.
8. Use a **REL.CE** command to relabel all 61 comparators of the network according to the poset shown in step 5.

References

1. Batcher KE, Al-Haj Baddar S (2008) Sortnet: a program for building faster sorting networks. Department of Computer Science, Kent State University, Kent, OH, USA, TR-KSU-CS-2008-01
2. Al-Haj Baddar S, Batcher KE (2009) Finding faster sorting networks using sortnet. VDM Publishing House Ltd., Germany
3. Cormen T, Leiserson C, Rivest R, Stein C (2001) Introduction to algorithms, 2nd edn. McGraw Hill Book Company, USA

Chapter 7
Divide and Conquer

In Chap. 5 we analyzed the 16-key sorting network that was discovered by David C. Van Voorhis and found out that it uses a divide-and-conquer strategy:

- As shown in Fig. 5.9 the first six steps of the sorting network partition the keys into four 4-key groups (at least for the odd 0/1-cases) with every key in each group less than or equal to every key in the next higher group—this reduces the problem of sorting 16 keys to sorting the four keys within each group;
- Steps 7 and 8 finish sorting the keys within each group for the odd 0/1-cases; and
- Step 9 sorts all the even 0/1-cases to complete the sort of all 16 keys.

Many algorithms (both serial algorithms and parallel algorithms) use the divide-and-conquer strategy and it makes sense to try to use it to construct new sorting networks for other numbers of keys.

Before considering divide-and-conquer strategies for building sorting networks it's best to define strangers.

7.1 Strangers

Assume that 0/1-case A has exactly j zeroes so A is sorted if and only if $K[x] = 0$ for all $x < j$ and $K[x] = 1$ for all $x \geq j$. If case A is not sorted then there are some keys out of place, we define:

- $K[x]$ to be a **Low-1** in case A if $x < j$ but $K[x] = 1$.
- $K[x]$ to be a **High-0** in case A if $x \geq j$ but $K[x] = 0$.
- $K[x]$ to be a **stranger** in case A if $K[x]$ is either a Low-1 or a High-0 in case A.

The following facts are easily shown:

- In every 0/1-case the number of Low-1 keys is the same as the number of High-0 keys.
- A 0/1-case is sorted if and only if it has no strangers.

S. W. Al-Haj Baddar and K. E. Batcher, *Designing Sorting Networks*,
DOI: 10.1007/978-1-4614-1851-1_7, © Springer Science+Business Media, LLC 2011

Fig. 7.1 A Divide and
Conquer Strategy in a Sorting
Network

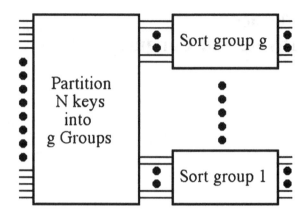

7.2   A Divide and Conquer Strategy

Figure 7.1 shows the basic block diagram of an N-key sorting network where the initial steps of the network partition the set of N keys into g groups and then the final steps sort the keys within each group.

What are the requirements that the initial partitioning steps must satisfy in order to get a successful partitioning of the N keys into g groups? Let's consider one of the groups, Group m, containing keys $K[i]$ through $K[k-1]$ as shown in Fig. 7.2 and a 0/1-case, A, with exactly j zeroes where $i < j < k$.

If the initial partitioning steps put any High-0 of case A into a group that's higher than Group m that High-0 will remain in that higher group so case A won't be sorted at the end of the sorting network.

Similarly, if the initial partitioning steps put any Low-1 of case A into a group that's lower than Group m that Low-1 will remain in that lower group so case A won't be sorted at the end of the sorting network.

To successfully partition case A, the initial steps must put all of its strangers into Group m. Section 4.4 shows that this can be accomplished if the initial partitioning steps completely sort certain bracket cases:

- all 0/1-cases with exactly i zeroes; and
- all 0/1-cases with exactly k zeroes.

Partitioning the N keys into g groups creates g-1 bracket cases which the initial partitioning steps must completely sort. Partitioning will probably require too many steps with this strategy so we should look for a better divide-and-conquer strategy.

Fig. 7.2 Group m Contains
Keys K[*i*] through K[*k*-1]

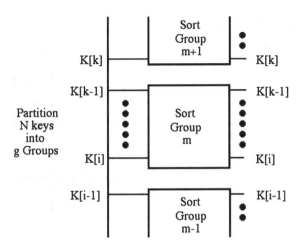

7.3 A Better Divide and Conquer Strategy

As shown in Fig. 5.8, the sorting network of Van Voorhis contains comparators
C(3,4), C(7,8), and C(11,12) in its last step which straddle the boundaries of the
sorted groups. These comparators reduce the requirements that the initial partitioning steps must satisfy for the bracket cases. For example, C(7,8) will sort the
cases with exactly 8 zeroes where the initial partitioning steps left a single Low-1
in the {K[4], K[5], K[6], K[7]} group and a single High-0 in the {K[8], K[9],
K[10], K[11]} group.

Figure 7.3 is like Fig. 7.2 except that comparators (labeled *M*) have been added
to straddle the boundaries between adjacent groups after the groups have been
sorted—each comparator compares the highest key of the lower group with
the lowest key of the higher group and exchanges them if they are out of order.
This reduces the burden on the initial partitioning steps—instead of having to
completely sort every bracket case, these steps are now allowed to leave a single
stranger in each of the groups adjacent to the bracket.

Figure 7.4 illustrates how the burden on the initial partitioning steps can be
further reduced by replacing the comparator of each straddle with a merge network
to merge the two lowest keys of the higher group with the two highest keys of the
lower group. The initial partitioning steps can now leave up to two strangers in
each of the groups adjacent to the bracket.

One can expand the merge networks some more to further reduce the burden on
the initial partitioning steps. If a merge network merges the lowest *h* keys in its
higher group with the highest *h* keys in its lower group then the initial partitioning
steps can leave up to *h* High-0 keys in the higher group and up to *h* Low-1 keys in
the lower group.

Doubling the size of a merge network adds another level of comparators to it.
This will add another step to the whole sorting network unless the comparators in

Fig. 7.3 Straddling the
Boundaries of the Sorted
Groups

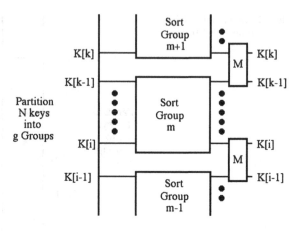

Fig. 7.4 Expanding the
Straddling with Merge
Networks

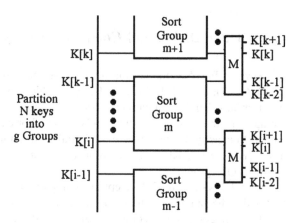

the merge network can use the same steps as the final steps in the group-sorting
networks. If we examine the sorting network in Figs. 49 and 51 of [1] we notice
that every one of them sorts a number of their lowest keys and highest keys before
sorting their keys in the center. This allows some of the comparators of a merge
network to share the same steps as the final steps in the group-sorting networks.

7.4 A Strategy For Designing Fast Sorting Networks

Here we present a strategy that one might use to design a fast N-key sorting
network—hopefully a network that uses less steps than any other previously-
known N-key network.

- (1)—Start with some comparator steps that connect the N keys together into a one-segment poset. Use Theorem 3-1 in Chap. 3 of these notes to preserve as many of the partial-orderings as possible.
- (2)—Examine the poset created by the comparators of (1) and change the comparators to re-label the keys of the poset in a logical order.
- (3)—Define the number of keys in each of the groups. This and the following steps may have to be repeated several times to get the best set of groups.
- (4)—If there are g groups defined then select g-1 brackets. For each group except the lowest group there is a bracket with exactly i zeroes where $K[i]$ is the lowest key in that group. The bracket separates keys in that group from keys in the next-lower group.
- (5)—For each bracket count the maximum number of strangers in each of the groups. Strangers that are in the two groups separated by the bracket are Near-Strangers and strangers that are in groups farther away from the bracket are Far-Strangers.
- (6)—Add partitioning steps to eliminate all Far-Strangers of all brackets. Compare each Far-Stranger with the key that eliminates it for the largest number of 0/1-cases.
- (7)—Examine the maximum number of Near-Strangers for each bracket. If the maximum number is small the Near-Strangers can be treated with merge networks after the keys in each group are sorted. If the maximum number of Near-Strangers is large it's probably best to eliminate some of them with comparators in the partitioning steps.
- (8)—Count the number of steps in the whole sorting network (including the steps in the merges after the groups are sorted.) If the number looks too large one may want to go back to step (3) and define a different set of groups.

Reference

1. Knuth D (1998) The art of computer programming: volume 3 sorting and searching, 2nd edn. Addison-Wesley Longman, USA, pp 225–228

Chapter 8
Counting Strangers

Section 7.4 describes a strategy for designing fast sorting networks. In step (5) of that strategy the maximum number of strangers in each group must be found for each bracket case. A new command, **SHOW.STRNGR.CNTS**, was added to the Sortnet program to perform this step.

8.1 SHOW.STRNGR.CNTS

The Sortnet command to count strangers is **SHOW.STRNGR.CNTS**—as with all the other Sortnet commands, you can substitute some other mnemonic for this command in your **EQUIV.LST**.

The command has no arguments since a user should precede it with a **SEL.CASES** command to define the bracket cases. Defining b bracket cases defines $b + 1$ groups. For an N-key network, if the bracket cases are the 0/1-cases with exactly: $z_1, z_2, ..., z_b$ zeroes, then:

- the first group contains keys K[0], K[1], ..., K[z_1-1];
- the second group contains keys K[z_1], K[$z_1 + 1$], ..., K[z_2-1];
- the third group contains keys K[z_2], K[$z_2 + 1$], ..., K[z_3-1];
- and so on;
- so the last group contains keys K[z_b], K[$z_b + 1$], ..., K[$N-1$]. Note that **SHOW.STRNGR.CNTS** assumes each group contains adjacent keys so one should re-label the keys to put them in this order.

For each bracket, **SHOW.STRNGR.CNTS** examines every 0/1-case with exactly the number of specified zeroes and finds how many strangers are in each of the groups. Some cases may have no zeroes in a particular group and other cases may have several strangers in the same group. Since a sorting network should sort *all* cases [1, 2], **SHOW.STRNGR.CNTS** picks the worst-case (the case with the most strangers in a particular group).

S. W. Al-Haj Baddar and K. E. Batcher, *Designing Sorting Networks*,
DOI: 10.1007/978-1-4614-1851-1_8, © Springer Science+Business Media, LLC 2011

Fig. 8.1 The Stranger Counts after Step 4

```
WORST-CASE STRANGER COUNTS
   Number of Zeroes
   in Bracket Cases
   1   5   8  11  15
   0   0   0   0   0  Group:  0
   0   1   1   0   0  Group:  1  2  3  4
   0   1   3   1   0  Group:  5  6  7
   0   1   3   1   0  Group:  8  9 10
   0   0   1   1   0  Group: 11 12 13 14
   0   0   0   0   0  Group: 15
```

Fig. 8.2 The Stranger Counts after Step 6 with 5 Brackets

```
WORST-CASE STRANGER COUNTS
   Number of Zeroes
   in Bracket Cases
   1   5   8  11  15
   0   0   0   0   0  Group:  0
   0   1   1   0   0  Group:  1  2  3  4
   0   1   1   0   0  Group:  5  6  7
   0   0   1   1   0  Group:  8  9 10
   0   0   1   1   0  Group: 11 12 13 14
   0   0   0   0   0  Group: 15
```

For b brackets, **SHOW.STRNGR.CNTS** displays a table with b columns and $b + 1$ rows—each entry in the table shows the maximum number of strangers in the corresponding group for the corresponding bracket.

8.2 Example: Counting Strangers in the Sorting Network of Chapter 5

Figure 5.8 shows the last 5 steps of the re-labeled 16-key sorting network analyzed in Chap.5. We generate 0/1-cases based on the first four steps of the re-labeled network; select five brackets with: **SEL.CASES 1 5 8 11 15**; and then issue a **SHOW.STRNGR.CNTS** to display the table shown in Fig. 8.1.

When we generate 0/1-cases based on the first six steps of the re-labeled network and use the same five brackets, **SHOW.STRNGR.CNTS** displays the table shown in Fig. 8.2.

When we change the brackets with **SEL.CASES 4 8 12**, then **SHOW.STRNGR.CNTS** displays the table shown in Fig. 8.3.

Fig. 8.3 The Stranger
Counts after Step 6 with 3
Brackets

```
WORST-CASE STRANGER COUNTS

Number of Zeroes
in Bracket Cases
  4   8  12
  1   0   0  Group:  0  1  2  3
  1   1   0  Group:  4  5  6  7
  0   1   1  Group:  8  9 10 11
  0   0   1  Group: 12 13 14 15
```

8.3 Matching Strangers

Section 7.4 describes a strategy for designing fast sorting networks. In steps (6) and (7) of that strategy comparators are added to the CL that compare some of the strangers with other keys to try and eliminate them. What other key should a given stranger be compared with? We conjecture that the best choice is the key that eliminates the stranger in the largest number of 0/1-cases . A new command, **SHOW.MATCHES**, was added to the Sortnet program to help make these choices.

SHOW.MATCHES

The Sortnet command to count strangers is **SHOW.MATCHES**—as with all the other sortnet commands, you can substitute some other mnemonic for this command in your **EQUIV.LST**. The command has no arguments since a user should precede it with a SEL.CASES command to define the bracket cases.

For each key, H, **SHOW.MATCHES** counts the number of bracket cases where that key is a High-0. Also, for every key, L where $L < H$, it counts the number of cases where H is a High-0 and L has a 1-value—these are the cases where comparator $C(L,H)$ would eliminate the High-0.

Similarly, for each key, L, **SHOW.MATCHES** counts the number of bracket cases where that key is a Low-1. Also, for every key, H where $H > L$, it counts the number of cases where L is a Low-1 and H has a 0-value —these are the cases where comparator $C(L,H)$ would eliminate the Low-1.

SHOW.MATCHES first displays these counts for the High-0's and then for the Low-1's. Each display first lists the keys with the number of cases where the key is a High-0 or a Low-1. Then a two-dimensional table is displayed with a column for each stranger (High-0 or Low-1) and a row for each key that could be used in a comparator to possibly eliminate the stranger. The numbers in the two-dimensional table are percentages; e.g., in the High-0 display the number in column H and row L shows the percentage of those cases where H is a High-0 that $C(L,H)$ will eliminate the High-0.

For a given stranger, the best choice for a comparator would be the row with the highest percentage in its column.

HIGH-0's FOR BRACKETS: 8	LOW-1's FOR BRACKETS: 8
8 is a High-0 in 12 cases.	1 is a Low-1 in 1 cases.
9 is a High-0 in 12 cases.	2 is a Low-1 in 1 cases.
10 is a High-0 in 12 cases.	3 is a Low-1 in 1 cases.
11 is a High-0 in 1 cases.	4 is a Low-1 in 1 cases.
12 is a High-0 in 1 cases.	5 is a Low-1 in 12 cases.
13 is a High-0 in 1 cases.	6 is a Low-1 in 12 cases.
14 is a High-0 in 1 cases.	7 is a Low-1 in 12 cases.

	8	9	10	11	12	13	14
1:	0	8	8	0	0	0	100
2:	8	0	8	0	0	100	0
3:	8	8	0	0	100	0	0
4:	0	0	0	100	0	0	0
5:	58	58	66	0	0	100	100
6:	58	66	58	0	100	0	100
7:	66	58	58	0	100	100	0
8:	0	58	58	100	0	0	100
9:	0	0	58	100	0	100	0
10:	0	0	0	100	100	0	0
11:	0	0	0	0	100	100	100
12:	0	0	0	0	100	100	0
13:	0	0	0	0	0	0	100

	1	2	3	4	5	6	7
2:	100	0	0	0	0	0	0
3:	100	100	0	0	0	0	0
4:	100	100	100	0	0	0	0
5:	0	0	100	100	0	0	0
6:	0	100	0	100	58	0	0
7:	100	0	0	100	58	58	0
8:	0	100	100	0	58	58	66
9:	100	0	100	0	58	66	58
10:	100	100	0	0	66	58	58
11:	0	0	0	100	0	0	0
12:	0	0	100	0	0	8	8
13:	0	100	0	0	8	0	8
14:	100	0	0	0	8	8	0

Fig. 8.4 The SHOW.MATCHES Displays

8.4 Example: Matching Strangers in the Sorting Network of Chapter 5

Figure 5.8 shows the last 5 steps of the re-labeled 16-key sorting network analyzed in Chap.5. We generate 0/1-cases based on the first four steps of the re-labeled network; select one bracket with: **SEL.CASES 8**; and then issue a **SHOW.MATCHES** command to display the counts. Figure 8.4 shows the displays for the High-0's and the Low-1's.

We ignore the Strangers in keys 1, 2, 3, 4, 11, 12, 13, and 14 because Fig. 5.8 shows these keys being sorted in boxes A and D.

The High-0's display shows us that key 8 is a High-0 in twelve of the bracket cases and the same is true for keys 9 and 10. The two-dimensional table tells us that matching key 7 with 8, matching key 6 with 9, and matching key 5 with 10 eliminates these High-0's in the most cases.

The Low-1's display shows us that key 5 is a Low-1 in twelve of the bracket cases and the same is true for keys 6 and 7. The two-dimensional table tells us that matching key 7 with 8, matching key 6 with 9, and matching key 5 with 10 eliminates these Low-1's in the most cases.

Fig. 8.5 Straddling the boundaries of the sorted groups

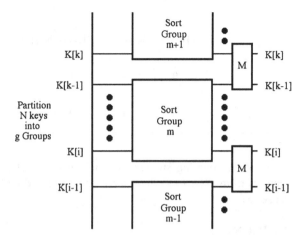

Fortunately, there is no conflict between the best matches—comparators C(7,8), C(6,9), and C(5,10) will eliminate the High-0's and the Low-1's in most of the cases. Figure 5.8 shows us that these are same comparators that are used in Step 5 of the network.

8.5 A Problem With SHOW.STRNGR.CNTS

This section shows a problem with the **SHOW.STRNGR.CNTS** command in Sortnet and describes a new command, **SHOW.CNTS.PM1**, which should be used instead of **SHOW.STRNGR.CNTS**.

The Problem

Figure. 8.5 is a copy of Fig. 7.3 which shows comparators (labeled M) straddling the boundaries of the sorted groups of keys to compare/exchange the highest key in each group with the lowest key in the next higher group.

Each M-comparator in the figure completes the sort of a particular bracket case. For example, the M-comparator comparing $K[i]$ with $K[i-1]$ swaps those two keys if a 0/1-case with exactly i zeroes has a single High-0 in Group m and a single Low-1 in Group $m-1$.

The Sortnet **SHOW.STRNGR.CNTS** command counts strangers for the group -bracket cases; e.g., 0/1-cases with exactly i zeroes and with exactly k zeroes in Fig. 8.5. It doesn't count strangers for 0/1-cases *between* the group brackets.

Sorting the group -bracket cases with the M-comparators does not guarantee that all other 0/1-cases are also sorted. For example, consider a case with exactly $i + 1$ zeroes that has a Low-1 in group $m-1$ and an extra 0 in group m as shown in the second row of the following table:

...	K[i-3]	K[i-2]	K[i-1]	K[i]	K[i+1]	K[i+2]	K[i+3]	..
...	0	0	1	0	0	1	1	..
...	0	0	0	1	0	1	1	..

Instead of counting strangers for the group-bracket cases it's better to count strangers from 0/1-cases which have one more and one less zero than the group-bracket cases.

SHOW.CNTS.PM1

SHOW.CNTS.PM1 stands for Show-Stranger-Counts-Plus/Minus-One. It's best described by repeating the example in Sect.8.4.

Figure 5.8 shows the last 5 steps of the re-labeled 16-key sorting network analyzed in Chap.5. We generate 0/1-cases based on the first four steps of the re-labeled network; select five brackets with: **SEL.CASES 1 5 8 11 15**; and then use a **SHOW.STRNGR.CNTS** to display the table shown in Fig. 8.6.

Figure 8.7 shows the table displayed by **SHOW.CNTS.PM1** if it is used instead of **SHOW.STRNGR.CNTS**:

The two displays differ in three ways:

- There are more columns in the SHOW.CNTS.PM1 display because each column of the SHOW.STRNGR.CNTS display is replaced by two columns with one less zero and with one more zero (SHOW.CNTS.PM1 deletes any column with no zeroes or with all zeroes because these cases have no strangers.)
- The order of the rows is reversed so the higher groups are above the lower groups. This puts all High-0 counts above the Low-1 counts.
- For each column the SHOW.CNTS.PM1 display shows a pair of hyphens, --, in the group that can't contain any stranger to separate the High-0 counts from the Low-1 counts.

SHOW.CASES

Another command added to Sortnet—**SHOW.CASES** shows every 0/1-case in the set of cases generated by **GEN.CASES**. Near the beginning of a sorting network there might be hundreds or thousands of cases so **SHOW.CASES** won't tell you much. Near the end of a sorting network there should be only a few 0/1-cases so **SHOW.CASES** will show you which cases are sorted and which cases are not sorted.

To save space, each 0/1-case is displayed with up to 8 hexadecimal digits instead of with up to 32 binary bits. The rightmost hexadecimal digit indicates the bits in K[3], K[2], K[1], and K[0]. The leftmost hexadecimal digit indicates the bits in the highest keys, $K[N-1]$, $K[N-2]$, ...

Fig. 8.6 The
SHOW.STRNGR.CNTS
display

WORST-CASE STRANGER COUNTS

Number of Zeroes
in Bracket Cases

1	5	8	11	15					
0	0	0	0	0	Group:	0			
0	1	1	0	0	Group:	1	2	3	4
0	1	3	1	0	Group:	5	6	7	
0	1	3	1	0	Group:	8	9	10	
0	0	1	1	0	Group:	11	12	13	14
0	0	0	0	0	Group:	15			

WORST-CASE STRANGER COUNTS WITH +1/-1 BRACKETS
Number of Zeroes in 0/1-Cases

2	4	6	7	9	10	12	14					
0	0	0	0	0	0	0	0	Group:	15			
0	0	0	0	1	1	--	--	Group:	11	12	13	14
0	1	2	2	--	--	1	0	Group:	8	9	10	
0	1	--	--	2	2	1	0	Group:	5	6	7	
--	--	1	1	0	0	0	0	Group:	1	2	3	4
0	0	0	0	0	0	0	0	Group:	0			

Fig. 8.7 The SHOW.CNTS.PM1 display

The hex-digits for up to eight cases are shown on each line of the display. First all cases with no zeroes are displayed, then all cases with one zero are displayed, etc. Blank lines in the display separate the cases with different numbers of zeroes.

References

1. Knuth D (1998) The art of computer programming: volume 3 sorting and searching, 2nd edn. Addison-Wesley Longman, USA, pp 225–228
2. Cormen T, Leiserson C, Rivest R, Stein C (2001) Introduction to algorithms, 2nd edn. McGraw-Hill Book Company, USA

Chapter 9
Finding Better Networks

We say that a new network for N keys is better than all other known networks for N keys if:

- it is more efficient (uses less comparators than all other N-key networks); or
- it is faster (uses less steps than all other N-key networks).

Note that most efficient sorting network for N keys might require more steps than a less efficient network. Section 9.1 describes what we know about the number of comparators in N-key networks for $N \leq 32$ and Sect. 9.2 describes what we know about the number of steps in N-key networks for $N \leq 32$.

9.1 The Number of Comparators

What is the best we can do in reducing the number of comparators in an N-key network? We can't do any better than the *information-theoretic lower bound* [1, 2]—each comparator only has two states (exchange or don't exchange) and an N-key sorting network must sort all $N!$ permutations of N distinct keys so the number of comparators must be at least ceil($\log_2(N!)$).

But unlike other comparison-sort algorithms (e.g., Quicksort and Heapsort), a sorting network is *oblivious*—whether some comparison, $C(i, j)$, decides to exchange $K[i]$ with $K[j]$ or not; every later comparator in the network compares keys in the same locations. This fact raises the lower bound in some cases—e.g., the lower bounds for $N = 5, 6, 7$, and 8 are 9, 12, 16, and 19, respectively, instead of the information-theoretic lower bounds of 7, 10, 13, and 16.

Table 9.1 shows what we know about the number of comparators in sorting networks for $1 \leq N \leq 16$. The second row shows the number of comparators in the most efficient network known so far and the third row shows the best lower bound known so far. Note that for $9 \leq N \leq 16$, there is a difference between the second row and the third row—either there exists a better N-key network that uses fewer comparators or there is a greater lower bound.

S. W. Al-Haj Baddar and K. E. Batcher, *Designing Sorting Networks*,
DOI: 10.1007/978-1-4614-1851-1_9, © Springer Science+Business Media, LLC 2011

Table 9.1 [3]

N	1	2	3	4	5	6	7	8	9	10	11	12	13	14	15	16
Most efficient	0	1	3	5	9	12	16	19	25	29	35	39	45	51	56	60
Best lower bound	0	1	3	5	9	12	16	19	20	22	26	29	33	37	41	45

Table 9.2 [3]

N	17	18	19	20	21	22	23	24	25	26	27	28	29	30	31	32
Most efficient	73	80	88	93	103	110	118	123	133	140	150	157	166	172	180	185
Best lower bound	49	53	57	62	66	70	75	80	84	89	94	98	103	108	113	118

Table 9.2 shows what we know about the number of comparators in sorting networks for $17 \leq N \leq 32$. The most efficient network for these values of N sorts floor($N/2$) keys and ceil($N/2$) keys using the most efficient networks in Table 9.1 and then merges these two sorted lists using an odd–even merge. It is worth mentioning that a difference between the second row and the third row exists for all values of N in this table. Thus, either there exists a better N-key network that uses fewer comparators or there is a greater lower bound.

9.2 The Number of Steps

What is the best we can do in reducing the number of steps in an N-key network?

If the input size is even, then the maximum number of comparators that can be put in each step is $N/2$. Let $S(N)$ denote the best lower bound on the number of comparators for an N-key network, then the smallest number of steps will be ceil($S(N)/(N/2)$). Also, if the input size is odd, then each step will be able to accommodate up to $(N - 1)/2$ comparators. If $S(N)$ is the best lower bound on the number of comparators for an N-key network, then sorting cannot complete in less than ceil($S(N)/((N - 1)/2)$) steps.

But we know that the lower bound on the number of steps for an N-key network can't be less than the best lower bound on the number of steps for an $(N - 1)$-key network. For example, if $N = 6$ then $S(N) = 12$ from Table 9.1 and $N/2 = 3$ so we get 4 for a lower bound on the number of steps of a 6-key network. But if $N = 5$ then $S(N) = 9$ from Table 9.1 and $(N - 1)/2 = 2$ so we get 5 for a lower bound on the number of steps of a 5-key network. This means that the lower bound on the number of steps of a 6-key network must also be 5.

Table 9.3 shows what we know about the number of steps in sorting networks for $1 \leq N \leq 16$ [3]. The number of steps in the fastest network known so far is depicted in the second row, whereas the third row shows the best lower bound known so far. Again, there is a gap between the second row and the third row for

Table 9.3 [3]

N	1	2	3	4	5	6	7	8	9	10	11	12	13	14	15	16
Fastest	0	1	3	3	5	5	6	6	7	7	8	8	9	9	9	9
Best lower bound	0	1	3	3	5	5	6	6	7	7	7	7	7	7	7	7

Table 9.4 The fastest-known networks for input sizes ranging between 17 and 32 together with their theoretic lower bounds

N	17*	18*	19	20	21*	22*	23	24	25	26	27	28	29	30	31	32
Fastest	11	11	12	12	12	12	13	13	14	14	14	14	14	14	14	14
Best lower bound	7	7	7	7	7	7	7	7	7	7	8	8	8	8	8	8

$11 \leq N \leq 16$. So, either a better N-key network that uses fewer steps can be designed or there is a greater lower bound.

Table 9.4 shows what we know about the number of steps in sorting networks for $17 \leq N \leq 32$. The fastest network for these values of N is to sort floor($N/2$) keys and ceil($N/2$) keys using the fastest networks in Table 9.3 and then to merge these two sorted lists using an odd–even merge. However, for $N = 17, 18, 21$, and 22(marked with a * in Table 9.4) a different strategy was used. An 11-step 18-key network and a 12-step 22-key network were discovered using Sortnet as described in [3]. These two networks are each one step faster than the corresponding merge-sorting networks. This discovery helped find two faster networks for $N = 17$ and for $N = 21$ as well. The reader may refer to Chap. 17 for more details.

References

1. Cormen T, Leiserson C, Rivest R, Stein C (2001) Introduction to algorithms, 2nd edn. McGraw-Hill Book Company, USA
2. Brassard G, Bratley P (1996) Fundamentals of algorithmics. Prentice Hall, Englewood Cliffs
3. Al-Haj Baddar S, Batcher KE (2009) Finding faster sorting networks using sortnet. VDM Publishing House Ltd., Germany

Chapter 10
Lattice Theory

In Chap. 3 we described the process of sorting N keys in a sorting network in terms of partially-ordering the set of keys. In formal terms, a *partially-ordered set* (or *poset*) is a set in which a binary relation $x \leq y$ is defined which satisfies for all x, y, and z in the set:

- For all x, $x \leq x$.
- If $x \leq y$ and $y \leq x$, then $x = y$.
- If $x \leq y$ and $y \leq z$, then $x \leq z$.

10.1 Isotone Functions

Given two posets, X and Y, we say that f is a function from X to Y if for every x in X, $f(x)$ is in Y. If X contains $|X|$ elements and Y contains $|Y|$ elements then there are $|Y|^{|X|}$ different functions from X to Y [1]. As examples, Let P and Q be the posets diagramed in Figs. 10.1 and 10.2, respectively.

Then there are $3^2 = 9$ different functions from P to Q as shown in Fig. 10.3 and $2^3 = 8$ different functions from Q to P as shown in Fig. 10.4.

We say that a function from a poset X to a poset Y is *isotone* or *order-preserving* if for every x_1 and x_2 in X, if $x_1 \leq x_2$ in X then $f(x_1) \leq f(x_2)$ in Y [1].

As examples, of the nine functions from P to Q shown in Fig. 10.3, only the five shown in Fig. 10.5 are isotone and of the eight functions from Q to P shown in Fig. 10.4, only the five shown in Fig. 10.6 are isotone.

S. W. Al-Haj Baddar and K. E. Batcher, *Designing Sorting Networks*, 61
DOI: 10.1007/978-1-4614-1851-1_10, © Springer Science+Business Media, LLC 2011

Fig. 10.1 Poset P

Fig. 10.2 Poset Q

Fig. 10.3 Functions from P
to Q

```
                              f(a)  f(b)
                              ---------
                               c     c
                               c     d
                               c     e
                               d     c
                               d     d
                               d     e
                               e     c
                               e     d
                               e     e
```

Fig. 10.4 Functions from Q
to P

```
                         f(c)  f(d)  f(e)
                         ---------------
                          a     a     a
                          a     a     b
                          a     b     a
                          a     b     b
                          b     a     a
                          b     a     b
                          b     b     a
                          b     b     b
```

Fig. 10.5 Isotone Functions
from P to Q

```
                              f(a)  f(b)
                              ---------
                               c     c
                               c     e
                               d     d
                               d     e
                               e     e
```

Fig. 10.6 Isotone Functions
from Q to P

```
                         f(c)  f(d)  f(e)
                         ---------------
                          a     a     a
                          a     a     b
                          a     b     b
                          b     a     b
                          b     b     b
```

10.2 Combining Posets

Combining posets together can be achieved using the three cardinal arithmetic operations: cardinal sum, cardinal product, and cardinal power.

Cardinal Sum: Assume that X and Y are disjoint posets, then the *cardinal sum* of X and Y, denoted by $X + Y$, is the set of all elements that exist either in X or Y in where:

- If x_1 and x_2 exist in X where $x_1 \leq x_2$, then $x_1 \leq x_2$ in $X + Y$.
- If y_1 and y_2 exist in Y where $y_1 \leq y_2$, then $y_1 \leq y_2$ in $X + Y$.
- If x exists in X and y exists in Y then neither $x \leq y$ nor $y \leq x$ belongs to $X + Y$.

Putting the diagrams of X and Y next to each other results in the diagram of $X + Y$. For example, if Figs. 10.1 and 10.2 are the diagrams of posets P and Q, then Fig. 10.7 is the diagram for $P + Q$.

$X + Y$ contains as many as $|X| + |Y|$ elements.

Cardinal Product: If X and Y are disjoint posets, the *cardinal product* of X and Y, denoted by XY, is the set of all couples (x, y) where x is an element of X and y is an element of Y where $(x_1, y_1) \leq (x_2, y_2)$ if and only if $x_1 \leq x_2$ in X and $y_1 \leq y_2$ in Y [1]. Consequently, XY has as many as $|X| * |Y|$ elements. For example, if Figs. 10.1 and 10.2 are the diagrams of posets P and Q, then Fig. 10.8 is the diagram for PQ.

Cardinal Power: If Y and X are disjoint posets, then the *cardinal power* with base Y and exponent X, denoted by Y^X, is the set of all isotone functions from X to Y partially ordered by letting $f \leq g$ mean that $f(x) \leq g(x)$ for all x in X [1]. As examples, if Figs. 10.1 and 10.2 are the diagrams of posets P and Q, respectively, then: the isotone functions from Q to P are listed in Fig. 10.6 and the diagram for P^Q is shown in Fig. 10.9; and the isotone functions from P to Q are listed in Fig. 10.5 and the diagram for Q^P is shown in Fig. 10.10.

Cardinal Arithmetic Identities: The following nine identities are true for any posets, X, Y, and Z [1].

1. $X + Y = Y + X$
2. $X + (Y + Z) = (X + Y) + Z$
3. $XY = YX$
4. $X(YZ) = (XY)Z$
5. $X(Y + Z) = XY + XZ$
6. $(X + Y)Z = XZ + YZ$
7. $X^{(Y + Z)} = X^Y X^Z$
8. $(XY)^Z = X^Z Y^Z$
9. $(X^Y)^Z = X^{YZ}$

Fig. 10.7 Poset P + Q

Fig. 10.8 Poset PQ

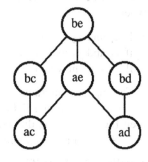

Fig. 10.9 Poset P^Q

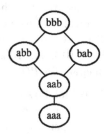

Fig. 10.10 Poset Q^P

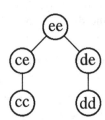

10.3 Joins and Meets

Assume that P is a poset and let x and y be any two elements in P. We say that z is an *upper bound* of x and y if [1, 2]:

- z is in P,
- $z \geq x$, and
- $z \geq y$.

Fig. 10.11 The joins of the elements in P^Q

$x\lor y$ in P^Q					
x	Y				
	aaa	aab	abb	bab	Bbb
aaa	aaa	aab	abb	bab	Bbb
aab	aab	aab	abb	bab	Bbb
abb	abb	abb	abb	bbb	Bbb
bab	bab	bab	bbb	bab	Bbb
bbb	bbb	bbb	bbb	bbb	Bbb

Fig. 10.12 The meets of the elements in P

$x\land y$ in P^Q					
x	Y				
	aaa	aab	abb	bab	Bbb
aaa	aaa	aaa	aaa	aaa	Aaa
aab	aaa	aab	aab	aab	Aab
abb	aaa	aab	abb	aab	Abb
bab	aaa	aab	aab	bab	Bab
bbb	aaa	aab	abb	bab	Bbb

We say that x and y have a *least upper bound* or *join*, denoted by $x\lor y$, if:

- $x\lor y$ is an upper bound of x and y, and
- for all z that are upper bounds of x and y, we have that $x\lor y \le z$.

Common synonyms for *least upper bound* and *join* are: *l.u.b.*, *set-union*, and *logical-or*.

Similarly, we say that w is a *lower bound* [1, 2] of x and y if:

- w is in P,
- $w \le x$, and
- $w \le y$.

We say that x and y have a *greatest lower bound* or *meet*, denoted by $x\land y$, if:

- $x\land y$ is a lower bound of x and y, and
- for all w that are lower bounds of x and y, we have that $x\land y \ge w$.

Common synonyms for *greatest lower bound* and *meet* are: *g.l.b.*, *set-intersection*, and *logical-and*.

It is easy to see that if $x \le y$ then $x\lor y = y$ and $x\land y = x$.

For example, the joins of the elements in poset P^Q (Fig. 10.9) are shown in the table of Fig. 10.11 and their meets are shown in the table of Fig. 10.12.

Fig. 10.13 The joins of the
elements in Q^P

$x \lor y$ in Q^P					
x	Y				
	cc	ce	ee	de	dd
cc	cc	ce	ee	ee	ee
ce	ce	ce	ee	ee	ee
ee	ee	ee	ee	ee	ee
de	ee	ee	ee	de	de
dd	ee	ee	ee	de	dd

Fig. 10.14 The meets of the
elements in Q^P

$x \land y$ in Q^P					
	Y				
x	cc	ce	ee	de	dd
cc	cc	cc	ee	-	-
ce	cc	ce	ee	-	-
ee	ee	ee	ee	ee	ee
de	-	-	ee	de	dd
dd	-	-	ee	dd	dd

As another example, the joins of the elements in poset Q^P (Fig. 10.10) are
shown in the table of Fig. 10.13.

But some of the element-pairs in Q^P do not have any meets as shown by the
dashes in the table of Fig. 10.14.

Identities for Join and Meet Operations [1]: If x, y, and z, are any elements in a
poset P then the join and meet operations satisfy the following laws whenever the
expressions referred to exist:

1. $x \land x = x$
2. $x \lor x = x$
3. $x \land y = y \land x$
4. $x \lor y = y \lor x$
5. $(x \land y) \land z = x \land (y \land z)$
6. $(x \lor y) \lor z = x \lor (y \lor z)$
7. $x \land (x \lor y) = x$
8. $x \lor (x \land y) = x$

Fig. 10.15 The boolean
lattice B [4]

10.4 Lattices

Definition We say that a poset, X, is a **lattice** [1–3] if every pair of elements, x and y, in X have a join, $x \vee y$, and a meet, $x \wedge y$.

As examples, posets P (Fig. 10.1) and P^Q (Fig. 10.9) are lattices. Posets Q (Fig. 10.2), $P + Q$ (Fig. 10.7), PQ (Fig. 10.8), and Q^P (Fig. 10.10), are not lattices.

Definition We say that a poset, X, is a **chain** if it is totally-ordered; i.e., for every pair of elements, x and y, in X, either $x \le y$ or $x \ge y$.

Every chain is a lattice.

Properties of Lattices [1]:

1. Every finite lattice has exactly one element, **O**, where $\mathbf{O} \le x$ for every x in the lattice.
2. Every finite lattice has exactly one element, **I**, where $\mathbf{I} \ge x$ for every x in the lattice.
3. If L and M are lattices then their cardinal product, LM is also a lattice.
4. If L is a lattice and P is a poset then the cardinal power, L^P, is also a lattice.
5. In any lattice, the join and meet operations are isotone: if $y \le z$ then $x \wedge y \le x \wedge z$ and $x \vee y \le x \vee z$.
6. In any lattice, we have the distributive inequality: $x \wedge (y \vee z) \ge (x \wedge y) \vee (x \wedge z)$.
7. In any lattice, we have the distributive inequality: $x \vee (y \wedge z) \le (x \vee y) \wedge (x \vee z)$.
8. In any lattice, we have the modular inequality: if $x \le z$ then $x \vee (y \wedge z) \le (x \vee y) \wedge z$.

10.5 0/1-Cases

Figure 10.15 shows the poset of Fig. 10.1 with element **a** relabeled with **0** and element **b** relabeled with **1**— since **1** > **0** in Boolean algebra we will call this poset **B** for Boolean-**B** is a chain. Thus, it is also a lattice [4].

```
/* STEP 1 */    0  1      2  3      4  5      6  7
/* STEP 2 */    0  2      1  3      4  6      5  7
/* STEP 3 */    1  2      5  6
/* STEP 4 */    1  6      2  5      0  7      3  4
```

Fig. 10.16 CL of bitonic merging example

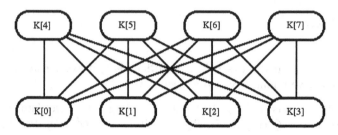

Fig. 10.17 Key-poset after bitonic merge example

Each 0/1-case for any poset X is just an isotone function from X to **B** so the poset of the 0/1-cases for a poset of keys, X, is just the cardinal power $\mathbf{B}^X$. By Property 4 of lattices we have that $\mathbf{B}^X$ is a lattice.

Assume that U (for unary) denotes the poset with exactly one element, u. Only two functions from U to $\mathbf{B}$: $f(u) = 0$ and $g(u) = 1$ exist. Notice that both functions are isotone with $f < g$ so $\mathbf{B}^U = \mathbf{B}$.

Note that if X is a chain of N elements then $\mathbf{B}^X$ is a chain of $(N+1)$ elements. The reader may refer to [4] for a detailed example on generating 0/1-case posets from regular key posets.

10.6 Bitonic Merging

In Sect. 4.5, we said that sometimes analyzing a poset of keys does not give us a complete picture of what's happening and mentioned that bitonic merging was an example. Here we will show an example of bitonic merging to prove that sometimes analyzing the 0/1-cases is better than analyzing the poset of keys. The example uses the Sortnet CL shown in Fig. 10.16. The first three steps sort keys K[0] through K[3] into order and sort keys K[4] through K[7] into order using two copies of Fig. 4.1 and then Step 4 performs the first step of a bitonic merge.

This CL partially orders the keys as shown in Fig. 10.17—the first step of the bitonic merge did indeed split the keys into two groups with the highest 4 keys in the higher group and the lowest 4 keys in the lower group.

```
/* STEP 1 */      0  4      1  5      2  6      3  7
/* STEP 2 */      0  5      1  6      2  7      3  4
/* STEP 3 */      0  6      1  7      2  4      3  5
/* STEP 4 */      0  7      1  4      2  5      3  6
```

Fig. 10.18 CL of direct comparisons

Fig. 10.19 Case-poset of
bitonic merging (in
Hexadecimal)

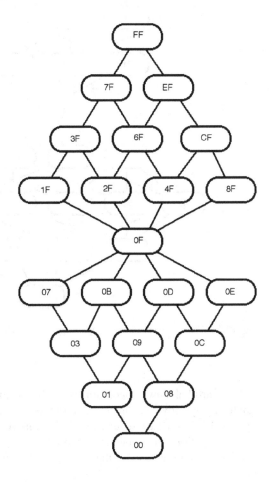

Another way to generate this same partial ordering of the keys is to use four
steps to directly compare each key in the lower group with each of the four keys in
the higher group as shown in the CL of Fig. 10.18.

Both CLs create the same partial ordering of the keys but Bitonic Merging
(Fig. 10.16) generates 21 cases with the partial-ordering shown in Fig. 10.19 while
Direct Comparisons (Fig. 10.18) generates 31 cases with the partial-ordering
shown in Fig. 10.20.

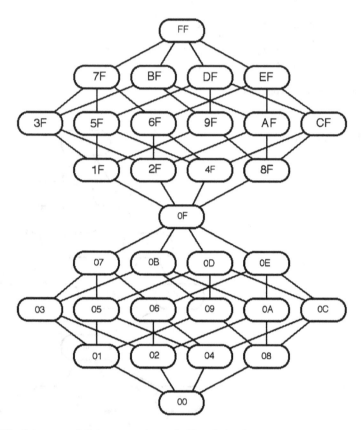

Fig. 10.20 Case-poset of direct comparisons (in Hexadecimal)

The Cardinal Power operation is well-defined so the same poset of the keys should always give us the same poset of the cases so why are the posets in Figs. 10.19 and 10.20 so different? The answer is that Sortnet operates in the reverse direction—first generating the set of 0/1-cases for a particular situation and then generating the poset of the keys from the set of 0/1-cases using the following rule:

- For all keys, K[x] and K[y], K[x] $\leq$ K[y] if there is *NO* 0/1-case where K[x] = 1 and K[y] = 0.

If we use the Cardinal Power operation to generate the poset of the 0/1-cases from the poset of the keys we obtain the 31-case poset of Fig. 10.20. Bitonic Merging deleted ten of these cases (because they were not bitonic) and left us with the 21-case poset of Fig. 10.19. The ten cases that were deleted did not add any new orderings to the keys so the poset of the keys remains the same.

References

1. Birkhoff G (1967) Lattice theory. American mathematical society, 3rd edn. Colloquium Publications, Providence
2. Rosen K (2003) Discrete mathematics and its applications, 5th edn. McGraw-Hill, USA
3. Grätzer GA (2003) General lattice theory. Birkhäuser, Switzerland
4. Al-Haj Baddar S, Batcher KE (2009) Finding faster sorting networks using sortnet. VDM Publishing House Ltd, Germany

Chapter 11
The AKS Sorting Network

After the publication of the 1968 paper, scholars noticed the difference between the $\Omega(\log^2 n)$ number of steps required by the merge-sorting networks and the lower bound of $O(\log n)$—either faster networks are possible or the lower-bound should be raised. In 1983, M. Ajtai, J. Komlos, and E. Szemeredi published two papers describing a sorting network that requires $C * \log n$ steps to sort n keys where C is a large constant—scholars usually refer to these sorting networks as the AKS networks [1, 2].

To describe the AKS networks we first describe *expander graphs*.

11.1 Expanders

A graph is *bipartite* if its set of vertices can be partitioned into two subsets, V_1 and V_2, such that every edge has one endpoint in V_1 and the other endpoint in V_2. For example Fig. 11.1 shows a bipartite graph with 8 vertices and 12 edges and Fig. 11.2 shows another bipartite graph with 10 vertices and 15 edges.

Given a subset U of V_1 or V_2 we let $\Gamma(U)$ be the subset of vertices in the other partition (V_2 or V_1) that are neighbors of vertices in U. In Fig. 11.1 for example, if $U = \{s_1\}$ then $\Gamma(U) = \{s_6, s_7, s_8\}$.

A bipartite graph with n vertices is a (d, ε)-*expander* if and only if:

1. the sets V_1 and V_2 each contain exactly $n/2$ vertices;
2. every vertex in V_1 and V_2 has exactly d neighbors; and
3. for every nonempty subset U in V_1 and for every nonempty subset U in V_2,

$$|\Gamma(U)| * \varepsilon \geq \min(\varepsilon * n/2, |U|) * (1 - \varepsilon),$$

where $0 < \varepsilon < 0.5$

As an example, Fig. 11.1 is a (3, 1/4)-expander with 8 vertices. Note that $\varepsilon * n/2 = 1$ and $(1 - \varepsilon)/\varepsilon = 3$. Any single vertex in V_1 or V_2 has three neighbors in

S. W. Al-Haj Baddar and K. E. Batcher, *Designing Sorting Networks*,
DOI: 10.1007/978-1-4614-1851-1_11, © Springer Science+Business Media, LLC 2011

Fig. 11.1 A (3, 1/4) expander [3]

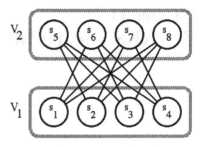

Fig. 11.2 A (3, 3/10) expander [3]

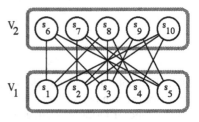

V_2 or V_1 so condition 3 is satisfied when $|U| = 1$. Any pair of vertices in V_1 or V_2 has four neighbors in V_2 or V_1 so condition 3 is also satisfied when $|U| > 1$.

As another example, Fig. 11.2 shows a (3, 3/10)-expander with 10 vertices. Note that $\varepsilon * n/2 = 1.5$ and $(1 - \varepsilon)/\varepsilon = 2.333$. Any single vertex in V_1 or V_2 has three neighbors in V_2 or V_1 so condition 3 is satisfied when $|U| = 1$. Any pair of vertices in V_1 or V_2 has at least four neighbors in V_2 or V_1 so condition 3 is also satisfied when $|U| > 1$.

Note that if $0 < \varepsilon < 0.5$ then for a sufficiently small subset U (i.e., when $|U| <= \varepsilon * n/2$) in one of the partitions, its neighborhood, $\Gamma(U)$, in the other partition is *expanded* by a factor of $(1 - \varepsilon)/\varepsilon > 1$. The expansion factor goes toward infinity as ε approaches 0.

The AKS networks use expanders with large numbers of vertices. It has been shown that for every $0 < \varepsilon < 0.5$, there exists some large constant d such that for sufficiently large n, (d, ε)-expanders can be found.

11.2 The Halver Circuit

Given n keys where n is even, an ε-halver will split the set of keys into a high-group and a low-group with $n/2$ keys in each group [3]. The split would be perfect if every key in the high-group is greater than every key in the low-group but the ε-halver may leave up to $\varepsilon * n$ keys in the wrong group. Given a (d, ε)-expander with n vertices, one can build an ε-halver using d steps with $n/2$ comparators in each step. The keys in the low-group correspond one-to-one with the vertices in V_1 of the expander and the keys in the high-group correspond one-to-one with the vertices in V_2. If s_i is any vertex in V_1 of the expander then, in each step of the

Fig. 11.3 A (1/4)-halver

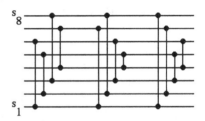

ε-halver, the key in the low-group corresponding to s_i is compared with the key in the high-group that corresponds to one of the neighbors of s_i in V_2.

As examples, Fig. 11.3 shows the (1/4)-halver built from the (3, 1/4)-expander of Figs. 11.1 and 11.4 shows the (3/10)-halver built from the (3, 3/10)-expander of Fig. 11.2.

If s_i is a vertex in V_1 then the ε-halver compares input s_i with the inputs corresponding to the d neighbors of s_i: exchanges occur whenever a neighbor has a lesser value so the value of s_i tends to decrease as it moves through the circuit. Similarly, if s_j is a vertex in V_2 then the value of input s_j tends to increase as it moves through the circuit.

An ε-halver tends to move the least $n/2$ values of the input sequence to outputs corresponding to vertices in V_1 and the greatest $n/2$ values of the input sequence to outputs corresponding to vertices in V_2.

How can we build a perfect halver? Make $d = n/2$ so every s_i in V_1 is compared with every s_j in V_2. Does d have to be that large? Yes. If $d < n/2$ then pick any s_i in V_1 and any s_j in V_2 that are not neighbors in the expander and suppose the input sequence is a 0/1-case with $s_i = 1$, $s_j = 0$, all other keys in $V_2 = 1$, and all other keys in $V_1 = 0$. The circuit will not perform any exchanges on this input sequence and leave s_i and s_j as strangers.

Is there an upper bound to the number of strangers in the output of an ε-halver? Yes. The number of strangers in V_1 must equal the number of strangers in V_2 and all neighbors of a stranger must be non-strangers. Let U be the set of all strangers in V_1 and let $k = |U|$. Then $|\Gamma(U)|$ cannot exceed $n/2 - k$. If $k > \varepsilon^* n/2$ then condition 3 of the (d, ε)-expander is not met so k is less than $\varepsilon^* n/2$ and the output of an ε-halver can have no more than $\varepsilon^* n$ strangers.

11.3 The Separator Circuit

Suppose one applies the V_1 output of an ε-halver (of size m) to a ε-halver (of size $m/2$) [3]. Let V_{11} and the V_{12} be the two halves of the output of the second ε-halver: $|V_{11}| = |V_{12}| = m/4$.

There are now two classes of strangers: *class-1-strangers* that are in the wrong half of the output of the first ε-halver and *class-2-strangers* that are in the correct half of the first output but in the wrong half of the output of the second ε-halver.

Fig. 11.4 A (3/10)-halver

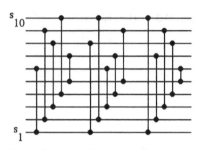

Let U be the set of class-1-strangers in V_{11}. Since every class-1-stranger really belongs in V_2 every element in $\Gamma(U)$ (in V_{12}) must also be a class-1-stranger. Since $|\Gamma(U)|/|U|$ is at least $(1 - \varepsilon)/\varepsilon$ and since V_1 contains at most $\varepsilon*m/2$ class-1-strangers we have that $|U|$ is at most $(\varepsilon)^2*m/2$.

Now let U be the set of class-2-strangers in V_{11}. Then $\Gamma(U)$ (in V_{12}) can't contain any class-2-stranger. Since $|\Gamma(U)|/|U|$ is at least $(1 - \varepsilon)/\varepsilon$ we have that $|U|$ is at most $\varepsilon*m/4$.

Suppose one now applies the V_{11} output to a third ε-halver (of size $m/4$). Let V_{111} and the V_{112} be the two halves of the output of the third ε-halver: $|V_{111}| = |V_{112}| = m/8$. We now have a third class of strangers: *class-3-strangers* that belong in V_{11} but are in the wrong half of V_{11}. Using the same arguments as before one can show that V_{111} contains at most:

$$(\varepsilon)^3 * m/2 \text{ class-1-strangers;}$$

$$(\varepsilon)^2 * m/2 \text{ class-2-strangers; and}$$

$$(\varepsilon) * m/8 \text{ class-3-srangers.}$$

A $(\lambda, \sigma, \varepsilon)$-*separator* circuit contains q levels of ε-halvers as shown in Fig. 11.5 [3]. It is obvious that $|A_1| = \lambda*m/2$ where $\lambda = 2^{(1-q)}$. By extending the foregoing arguments we have that A_1 contains at most:

$$(\varepsilon)^q * m/2 \text{ class-1-strangers;}$$

$$(\varepsilon)^{q-1} * m/4 \text{ class-2-strangers;}$$

$$\cdots$$

$$(\varepsilon) * m/2(2^q) \text{ class-q-strangers.}$$

The limits for the number of strangers of each class form a geometric sequence with q terms so the number of strangers of all classes in A_1 is at most: $\lambda*m*\varepsilon*f/2$ where $f = (1 - (2*\varepsilon)^q)/(1 - 2*\varepsilon) < q$. If we let $\sigma = q*\varepsilon$ then the number of strangers of all classes in A_1 is less than $\lambda*m*\sigma/2$.

The number of strangers of all classes in A_4 of Fig. 11.5 is also less than $\lambda*m*\sigma/2$. A $(\lambda, \sigma, \varepsilon)$-separator circuit contains q levels of ε-halvers and each ε-halver has a depth of d so the separator circuit has a constant depth of $q * d$.

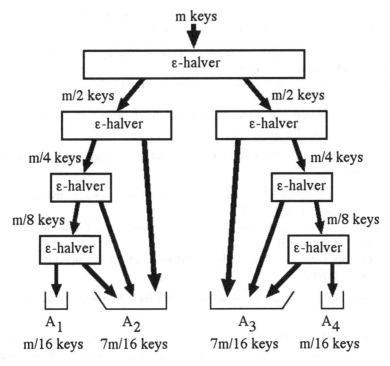

Fig. 11.5 A $(\lambda, \sigma, \varepsilon)$-separator

11.4 The Sorting Network

The sorting network has $O(\log n)$ layers with a complete binary tree on each layer with $O(n)$ nodes.

Each node of each tree contains one $(\lambda, \sigma, \varepsilon)$-separator circuit. To show how the separators are interconnected we index the nodes of each binary tree with the root being node 1 and every parent node i having nodes $2*i$ and $2*i + 1$ as children. Note that if $i > 1$ then the parent of node i is node $\lfloor i/2 \rfloor$. The following diagram illustrates the indexing method for a 4-level binary tree with 15 nodes:

node-1							
node-2				node-3			
node-4		node-5		node-6		node-7	
Node 8	Node 9	Node 10	Node 11	Node 12	Node 13	Node 14	Node 15

Figure 11.5 illustrates a separator receiving m inputs and separating them into four output groups, A_1, A_2, A_3, and A_4. If $i > 1$ then:

- output groups A_1 and A_4 of the separator in node-i on layer-j are fed into node-$(\lfloor\_i/2\_\rfloor)$ on the next layer, layer-$(j + 1)$;
- output group A_2 of the separator in node-i on layer-j is fed into node-$(2*i)$ on the same layer, layer-j; and
- output group A_3 of the separator in node-i on layer-j is fed into node-$(2*i + 1)$ on the same layer, layer-j.

The output groups of the separator at the root of each tree (node-1) are connected as follows:

- output groups A_1 and A_4 of the separator in node-1 on layer-j are fed into node-1 on the next layer, layer-$(j + 1)$;
- output group A_2 of the separator in node-1 on layer j is fed into node-2 on the same layer, layer-j; and
- output group A_3 of the separator in node-1 on layer j is fed into node-3 on the same layer, layer-j.

The sequence of n items to be sorted is fed into the separator in node-1 of layer-1.

The Action of a Node: To illustrate the action of a single node on a single layer in this sorting network we use node-10 on layer-1 as an example. The items sent into the separator of node-10 will be: non-strangers that really belong in node-10; low strangers that really belong in node-8 or node-9 and high strangers that really belong in node-11 through node-15. The separator in node-10 will tend to move low strangers to output group A_1 and high strangers to output group A_4.

In Fig. 11.5 what prevents a low stranger from being moved into output group A_1? In the chain of ε-halvers running toward group A_1 some halver routed the low stranger into another output group because *all* of the d neighbors of that stranger in that halver were also low strangers with even lower values. Each ε-halver in the chain routes most of the low strangers properly (toward A_1): if U is the set of low strangers routed improperly by a halver then $\Gamma(U)$ contains many more low strangers that are routed properly.

If node-10 receives g low strangers then output group A_1 receives at least $g*(1 - \varepsilon)^q$ low strangers (assuming the separator in node-10 has q levels of ε-halvers). Similarly, if node-10 receives h high strangers then output group A_4 receives at least $h*(1 - \varepsilon)^q$ high strangers.

Items in output groups A_1 and A_4 are routed to node-5 in layer-2 so all strangers found by node-10 are recycled back to the parent of node-10 in layer-2 to be processed again. Non-strangers and undiscovered strangers are routed to node-20 or node-21 in layer-1 for further splitting.

The Action of a Layer: Every node in a layer does a fairly good job of finding strangers that don't belong to that node and sending them to next layer to be processed again. Will every stranger eventually be discovered? Yes. The size of the separators decreases as one goes down the tree so at some level (within $O(\log n)$ levels) the size of every separator is $2*d$ and its halvers work perfectly.

Recycling Strangers: A stranger found in node-i on layer-j wound up in node-i because some ancestor node, node-k, routed it incorrectly. Somehow, the stranger must find its way back to a copy of node-k on some later level so that node can route it correctly.

For $i > 1$, strangers found by node-i in layer-j are routed to node-$(\lfloor i/2 \rfloor)$ in layer-$(j + 1)$; i.e., the copy of its parent node in the next layer. If that copy of the parent node finds the item to be a stranger then it will route the item to the copy of the grand-parent on the next level, etc., etc. Thus, the item will find its way back to a copy of the ancestor that routed it incorrectly provided that all intervening ancestors discover the item is a stranger. Should any intervening ancestor not make this discovery it will route the item to one of its children but eventually one of its descendants discovers its strangeness and starts routing the item back up toward a copy of node-k on another layer.

The Leaves of the Trees: One could continue the tree in each layer until the items on that layer are sorted but then the output of each layer would have to be merged with the outputs of other layers to complete the sort. A better scheme would be to send all items on each layer to copies of the nodes on the next layer at some point: all items will eventually collect in the last layer which will complete the sort.

11.5 Practicality Issues

Let the number of keys to be sorted, N, be a power of two.

An AKS sorting network requires $C \log_2(N)$ steps where C is some constant that nobody seems to know. Many believe that C is definitely in the hundreds and some even think it is in the thousands. Let us give the AKS networks the benefit of the doubt and assume that $C = 87$.

A merge-sorting network requires $\log_2(N) * (1 + \log_2(N))/2$ steps to sort N keys.

For very small N a Merge-sorting network requires less steps than an AKS sorting network and for very large N the opposite is true. Where is the cross-over point? That is, at what value of N do the two kinds of networks require the same number of steps? It's when $N = 2^{2C-1}$. If we assume that C is only 87 then the cross-over point is when $N = 2^{173} = 1.2 * 10^{52}$ [4]. An AKS network is faster than a merge-sorting network only when the number of keys is greater than $1.2 * 10^{52}$.

The mass of a proton is about $1.66 * 10^{-24}$ g and the mass of the earth is about $5.98 * 10^{24}$ kg so the earth has only about $3.6 * 10^{51}$ protons (and about the same number of electrons) [4]. Even if computer technology would ever advance to the point where each key can be stored in a single proton (or electron), a merge-sorting network is faster than an AKS network for any system that can be built on earth.

Remark   It's the usual practice, in the design and analysis of algorithms, to drop constant factors and just express execution time with order-of-magnitude notation. This practice is usually all right when analyzing sequential algorithms because execution time typically grows at least linearly with problem size. But the execution time of many parallel algorithms only grows logarithmically (or poly-logarithmically) with problem size. Constant factors become important.

References

1. Ajtai M, Komlos J, Szemeredi E (1983) Sorting in c log n steps. Combinatorica 3:1–19
2. Ajtai M, Komlos J, Szemeredi E (1983) An O(n log n) sorting network. In: Proceedings of the ACM symposium on theory of computing, pp 1–9
3. Akl SG (1997) Parallel computation: models and methods. Prentice-Hall, Upper Saddle River
4. Al-Haj Baddar S, Batcher KE (2009) Finding faster sorting networks using sortnet. VDM Publishing House Ltd., Germany

Chapter 12
Ideas for Faster Networks

Here are some ideas that you might find useful when trying to find an N-key sorting network that is faster than what is known so far. There is no guarantee that they always work but it might be fruitful to try some of them out to see if they do work in your situation.

12.1 Selecting N

What value of N should you select to try and find a faster N-key network? Selecting an even number for N is an obvious idea—if N is odd, then you can only put $(N-1)/2$ comparators in each step.

Table 9.3

N	1	2	3	4	5	6	7	8	9	10	11	12	13	14	15	16
Fastest	0	1	3	3	5	5	6	6	7	7	8	8	9	9	9	9
Best lower bound	0	1	3	3	5	5	6	6	7	7	7	7	7	7	7	7

Tables 9.3 and 9.4 from Chap. 9 are copied below. Select a value for N where the gap between the second and third row is large—the larger the gap the easier it might be to reduce the gap with a faster N-key network.

Table 9.4

N	17*	18*	19	20	21*	22*	23	24	25	26	27	28	29	30	31	32
Fastest	11	11	12	12	12	12	13	13	14	14	14	14	14	14	14	14
Best lower bound	7	7	7	7	7	7	7	7	7	7	8	8	8	8	8	8

If the size of the gap is the same for several values of N then select the least even N—it should be easier to find a faster network for a smaller value of N than for a larger value of N. As examples:

S. W. Al-Haj Baddar and K. E. Batcher, *Designing Sorting Networks*,
DOI: 10.1007/978-1-4614-1851-1_12, © Springer Science+Business Media, LLC 2011

- The gap is 7 for $N = 25$ or 26. Finding a faster 26-key sorting network should be easy because the gap is so large.
- The gap for $N = 21$ and $N = 22$ has become 5 instead of 6 (the reader may refer to Chap. 17 for more details).
- The gap is 6 for $N = 23$ and $N = 24$. Reducing the gap by finding a faster 22-key network turned out to be easier than finding a faster 24-key network.
- The gap is also 6 for $27 \leq N \leq 32$. Reducing the gap by finding a faster 28-key network is probably easier than finding a faster 30-key or 32-key network.
- The gap for $N = 17$ and $N = 18$ has become 4 instead of 5 (the reader may refer to Chap. 17 for more details).
- The gap is 5 for $N = 19$ and $N = 20$. Reducing the gap by finding a faster 18-key network turned out to be easier than finding a faster 20-key network.
- The gap is 2 for $13 \leq N \leq 16$. Reducing the gap by finding a faster 14-key network is probably easier than finding a faster 16-key network.
- The gap is 1 for $N = 11$ or 12. Finding a faster 12-key sorting network is probably very hard because the gap is so small.

When N is selected your first goal, **Goal1**, is one less than the number of steps in the fastest known network.

12.2 Starting Out

The initial steps of your network should combine all N keys into a single-segment poset[1]—analyzing 0/1-cases won't tell you much if the poset has two or more segments. There are two different ways you might try to minimize the number of steps this requires:

1. Analyze the initial steps of the network for $N/2$ keys to find out how many steps it takes to form a single-segment poset. Use the comparators in these steps to form the least $N/2$ keys of your network into a single-segment poset and another set of these comparators to form the greatest $N/2$ keys of your network into another single-segment poset. Then follow these steps with one step of comparators comparing corresponding keys of these two posets.
2. If $N > 16$ then use 5 steps to put 32 keys into a single-segment poset and then use CUT.CE.KEYS to cut out the least $(16-N/2)$ keys and the greatest $(16-N/2)$ keys of the 32 keys.
   If $N < 16$ then use 4 steps to put 16 keys into a single-segment poset and then use CUT.CE.KEYS to cut out the least $(8-N/2)$ keys and the greatest $(8-N/2)$ keys of the 16 keys.

From **Goal1** subtract the number of steps you take to start out to determine **Goal2**, the number of steps you can use for partitioning the keys into groups and for sorting the groups.

12.3 Sizes of Groups

In the divide-and-conquer strategy the final steps of your network will be a number of G-key sorting networks for some small G. It's best if G is even:

- sorting an odd number of keys requires as many steps as sorting the next higher even number of keys; and
- the last step doesn't touch the greatest and least keys of the group so that step can be used to eliminate strangers between adjacent groups.

From Table 9.3 we see that:

- sorting 4 keys requires 3 steps;
- sorting 6 keys requires 5 steps;
- sorting 8 keys requires 6 steps; and
- sorting 10 keys requires 7 steps.

You may have to try several different group sizes, G. The number of steps you can use for partitioning is:

Goal3 = **Goal2** − (number of steps to sort G keys.)

12.4 Placements of Groups

The hardest groups to partition are in the center of the N keys so concentrate on those groups for the moment. You have two choices:

1. Bracket cases: $N/2$-G, $N/2$, and $N/2 + G$; or
2. Bracket cases: $N/2$-$3G/2$, $N/2$-$G/2$, $N/2 + G/2$, and $N/2 + 3G/2$.

The first choice places one group just below the mid-point and the other just above the mid-point. The second choice places one group straddling the mid-point with another group just below it and a third group just above it.

Try both choices and try to partition the keys in the center using **Goal3** or less steps.

12.5 A Three-Phase Divide-and-Conquer Strategy

This strategy establishes a partial ordering relation among all keys via constructing a single-segment poset of N keys in L steps, where $L = \log N$, in the first phase. Afterwards, the keys get split into groups with the purpose of putting the keys that reside in the wrong group (strangers), back in their correct groups. Finally, each group gets sorted separately in the last phase. Occasionally, some comparisons between keys belonging to adjacent groups might be needed to finish the sorting

Fig. 12.1 A three-phase
technique for sorting

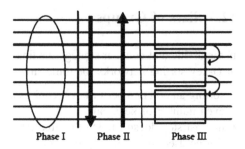

Phase I   Phase II   Phase III

process after the third phase, in a process called straddling group boundaries. Figure 12.1 illustrates this three-phase strategy.

The number of keys in each group must be significantly less than N and will be assumed to be $\sqrt{N}$. The following recurrence equation describes the number of steps, $S(N)$, it takes the proposed network to finish the sorting process:

$$S(N) = S(\sqrt{N}) + kL$$

where k is a constant

Solving the equation above results in $S(N)$ being $\theta(\log N)$, which implies the overall optimal sorting cost of $\theta(N \log N)$. However, if the second phase takes more than L steps, then a slightly longer implementation will be sought such that the network's overall sorting time will not exceed $\theta(N(\log N)(\log \log N))$.

12.6 Using Sortnet to Help Design Faster Networks

Sortnet is a vital tool for synthesizing and analyzing sorting networks. One can utilize Sortnet commands to help design faster sorting networks. Here we describe some strategies in which Sortnet is used to help design faster sorting networks.

Eliminating More Dashes from the Shmoo Chart

This strategy aims at picking pairs of CEs that minimize the number of dashes in the Shmoo chart (using the **SHOW.GOODCE** command). The reader can refer to Chaps. 16 and 17 for more details on this strategy.

Eliminating More Cases Using the Shmoo Chart

This strategy aims at utilizing the Shmoo chart in order to reduce the number of cases generated after comparing the selected pairs of elements. The keys that appear close to each other in a Shmoo chart tend to occupy same or nearby ranks in the corresponding poset. They also have relatively close number of cases for which their values are equal to 1. Thus, comparing such pairs of neighbor keys has been considered. Experimentation has shown that this strategy has been effective in reducing the number of resulting 0/1-cases.

Changing More Cases

This strategy aims at selecting the comparisons that affect the most 0/1-cases (using the **SHOW.DIFF** command). It is a conjecture that affecting more cases will help transform them into one of the $N + 1$ sorted cases faster and hence reduce the number of steps necessary to sort. Sortnet implements this strategy by counting the number of cases for which $K[x] > K[y]$ as well as $K[x] < K[y]$ for all x,y in $\{0,1,2,...,N\text{-}1\}$ and keeping the minimum count. Then, across all the counts kept, the pair of keys with the maximum count is selected.

Reference

1. Knuth D (1998) The art of computer programming: volume 3 sorting and searching, 2nd edn. Addison-Wesley Longman, USA, pp 225–228

Chapter 13
BOOL(N)

Let p be a positive integer and let $N = 2^p$. Here we describe a certain poset, which we call BOOL (N), of the N keys which has a number of special properties.

13.1 Building BOOL(N)

One can build BOOL (N) in p steps. If $p = 1$ then build BOOL(2) by using one comparator to compare K[0] with K[1]. If $p > 1$ then use the following algorithm recursively:

1. Use $p-1$ steps to build BOOL ($N/2$) out of the first $N/2$ keys, K[0] through K[$N/2-1$].
2. Use the same $p-1$ steps to build another BOOL ($N/2$) out of the last $N/2$ keys, K[$N/2$] through K[$N-1$].
3. Use one more step of $N/2$ comparators to compare K[i] with K[$i + N/2$] for $i = 0, 1, ..., N/2-1$.

As an example, Fig. 13.1 shows the Knuth diagram for building BOOL (16) in 4 steps.

Note that each step compares corresponding items of two different segments of a poset so it preserves information. We conjecture that this method of building a poset of $N = 2^p$ in p steps minimizes the number of 0/1-cases.

13.2 Poset Diagram For BOOL(N)

For all positive p the poset diagram for BOOL (N) has p dimensions. As examples, Figs. 13.2, 13.3, 13.4 and 13.5 show the poset diagrams for BOOL(2), BOOL(4), BOOL(8), and BOOL(16), respectively.

S. W. Al-Haj Baddar and K. E. Batcher, *Designing Sorting Networks*,
DOI: 10.1007/978-1-4614-1851-1_13, © Springer Science+Business Media, LLC 2011

Fig. 13.1 Building
BOOL(16) [1]

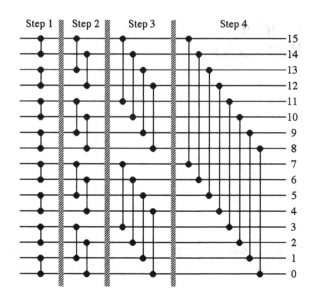

Fig. 13.2 BOOL(2)

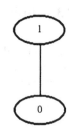

Fig. 13.3 3 BOOL(4)

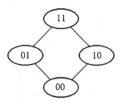

To simplify the description of the properties of BOOL (*N*) we label its keys with *p*-bit vectors instead of with integers.

Let *X*, *Y*, and *Z* be any three keys in BOOL (*N*), let $(x_1x_2...x_p)$ be the label of *X*, let $(y_1y_2...y_p)$ be the label of *Y*, and let $(z_1z_2...z_p)$ be the label of *Z*. Then:

1. $X \geq Y$ if and only if $x_k \geq y_k$ for all $k = 1, 2, ..., p$.
2. *X* covers *Y* if and only if $x_i > y_i$ for exactly one bit *i* in their labels and $x_k = y_k$ for all *k* not equal to *i*.

Fig. 13.4 BOOL(8)

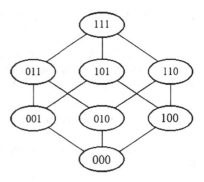

Fig. 13.5 BOOL(16)

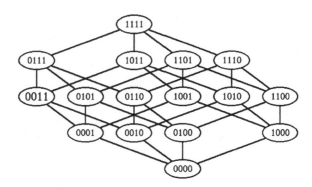

3. The meet of X and Y, $X \wedge Y$, is the key with label $(x_1 \wedge y_1, x_2 \wedge y_2, ..., x_p \wedge y_p)$.
4. The join of X and Y, $X \vee Y$, is the key with label $(x_1 \vee y_1, x_2 \vee y_2, ..., x_p \vee y_p)$.
5. Every pair of keys in BOOL (N) has a meet and a join so it is a lattice.
6. Let X be any key in BOOL (N), let $(x_1 x_2 ... x_p)$ be the label of X, and let X' be the only key in BOOL(N) with the complementary label $(x'_1 x'_2 ... x'_p)$. Then the meet of X and X', $X \wedge X'$, is the key with label $(00...0)$ and the join of X and X', $X \vee X'$, is the key with label $(11...1)$. We say that X' is the **complement** of X. BOOL(N) is a **complemented lattice** because every key has a unique complement.
7. The distributive laws:

   - $X \wedge (Y \vee Z) = (X \wedge Y) \vee (X \wedge Z)$
   - $X \vee (Y \wedge Z) = (X \vee Y) \wedge (X \vee Z)$
     hold for all keys, X, Y, and Z in BOOL (N) so it is a **distributive lattice**.

8. BOOL (N) is a complemented distributive lattice. It can be shown that every complemented distributive lattice must be a BOOL(N) for some $N = 2^p$ where p is a positive integer.

13.3 The Ranks of Keys in BOOL(N)

The N keys of BOOL (N) are grouped into $p + 1$ ranks where rank-k for k = 0, 1, 2, ..., p contains all keys with labels that have exactly k 1-bits and $(p-k)$ 0-bits. The number of keys in rank-k is $p!/(k!(p-k)!)$. The number of keys in rank-0 is 1 and for k = 0, 1, ..., $p-1$:

(the number of keys in rank-$(k + 1)$) = (the number of keys in rank-k) $(p-k)/(k + 1)$.

This formula can be used to calculate the number of keys in each of the ranks. For example, if $p = 9$, then:

k	Number of keys in rank-k	multiplier
0	1	
		9/1
1	9	
		8/2
2	36	
		7/3
3	84	
		6/4
4	126	
		5/5
5	126	
		4/6
6	84	
		3/7
7	36	
		2/8
8	9	
		1/9
9	1	

Another way to calculate the number of keys in each rank is with Pascal's Triangle [2] (Fig. 13.6). The number of keys in rank-k of BOOL (2^p) is the sum of:

- the number of keys in rank-$(k-1)$ of BOOL (2^{p-1}); and
- the number of keys in rank-k of BOOL (2^{p-1}).

13.4 Coverings

The label of each key in rank-k contains exactly k 1-bits and $(p-k)$ 0-bits. Let X be any key in rank-k and let $(x_1\ x_2...\ x_p)$ be the label of X.

Fig. 13.6 Pascal's Triangle
for p = 0, 1, 2, ..., 10

P	Pascal's Triangle	$N=2^p$
0	1	1
1	1 1	2
2	1 2 1	4
3	1 3 3 1	8
4	1 4 6 4 1	16
5	1 5 10 10 5 1	32
6	1 6 15 20 15 6 1	64
7	1 7 21 35 35 21 7 1	128
8	1 8 28 56 70 56 28 8 1	256
9	1 9 36 84 126 126 84 36 9 1	512
10	1 10 45 120 210 252 210 120 45 10 1	1024

- Let X cover Y where the label of Y is $(y_1 y_2 ... y_p)$. Then $y_k = x_k$ for all $k = 1$, $2, ..., p$, except that $y_i = 0$ and $x_i = 1$ for exactly one value of k. Since the label of X has exactly k 1-bits it covers exactly k keys in rank-$(k-1)$.
- Let Y cover X where the label of Y is $(y_1 y_2 ... y_p)$. Then $y_k = x_k$ for all $k = 1$, $2, ..., p$, except that $y_i = 1$ and $x_i = 0$ for exactly one value of k. Since the label of X has exactly $(p-k)$ 0-bits, X is covered by exactly $(p-k)$ keys in rank-$(k + 1)$.

13.5 Certain Subsets of BOOL(N)

Within BOOL (2^p) one can find many subsets that are copies of BOOL(2^q) for every $0 < q < p$. Let X and Y be any two keys in BOOL(2^p) where $X < Y$, let $(x_1 x_2 ... x_p)$ be the label of X, and let $(y_1 y_2 ... y_p)$ be the label of Y.

Since $X < Y$, if X is in rank-i, then Y must be in some higher rank, rank-$(i + d)$. When we compare corresponding bits in $(x_1 x_2 ... x_p)$ and $(y_1 y_2 ... y_p)$ we should find that the two labels agree in $(p-d)$ places and disagree in the other d places. In the d places where the two labels disagree the bit in $(x_1 x_2 ... x_p)$ must be 0 and the bit in $(y_1 y_2 ... y_p)$ must be 1.

Let Z be any key in BOOL (2^p) where $X \leq Z \leq Y$. The label of Z, $(z_1 z_2 ... z_p)$, must agree with the labels of X and Y in the same $(p-d)$ places where the labels of X and Y agree. In the d places where the labels of X and Y disagree, each bit of $(z_1 z_2 ... z_p)$ can be either 0 or 1. There are exactly 2^d keys, Z, where $X \leq Z \leq Y$, and the subset of BOOL(2^p) containing these keys is equivalent to BOOL(2^d).

Example: Let $p = 10$ and let X and Y be the two keys in BOOL (1024) with labels (0100111000) and (0101111011), respectively. X is in rank-4 and Y is in rank-7 so $d = 3$. The labels of X and Y agree in seven places, (010-1110- -), and disagree in the three places with hyphens (-). There are eight keys, Z, in BOOL(2^p) where $X \leq Z \leq Y$. Figure 13.7 shows these keys along with the corresponding keys in BOOL(8).

Fig. 13.7   (0100111000) < z
< (0101111011)

Z in BOOL (1024)	Corresponding Key in BOOL (8)
X = (0100111000)	(000)
(0100111001)	(001)
(0100111010)	(010)
(0100111011)	(011)
(0101111000)	(100)
(0101111001)	(101)
(0101111010)	(110)
Y = (0101111011)	(111)

13.6 GT(X), GE(X), LT(X) and LE(X)

If X is any key in any poset, P, then let:

- GT(X) be the number of keys in P that are known to be greater-than X;
- GE(X) be the number of keys in P that are known to be greater-than-or-equal-to X;
- LT(X) be the number of keys in P that are known to be less-than X; and
- LE(X) be the number of keys in P that are known to be less-than-or-equal-to X.

For all X, GE(X) = GT(X) + 1 and LE(X) = LT(X) + 1. Note that for every k in the first column of the table displayed by the SHOW.POSET command of Sortnet, GT(k) is displayed in the second column, and LT(k) is displayed in the third column.

GT(X) + LT(X) = $N-1$ if and only if key X is sorted. One measure of how close X is to being sorted is how close GT(X) + LT(X) is to $N-1$.

P = **BOOL** *(N)*: Let P = BOOL(N) where $N = 2^p$, let $0 \leq i \leq p$, and let X be any key in rank-i of BOOL(N):

- GE(X) is the number of keys greater-than-or-equal-to X and less-than-or-equal-to the maximum key of BOOL (N) in rank-p. From Sect. 13.5 we see that GE(X) = 2^{p-i}.
- LE(X) is the number of keys less-than-or-equal-to X and greater-than-or-equal-to the minimum key of BOOL (N) in rank-0. From Sect. 13.5 we see that LE(X) = 2^i.
- So GT(X) + LT(X) = $2^{p-i} + 2^i - 2$.

13.7 Depopulating BOOL(N)

This chapter shows that when $N = 2^p$, a good way to start building a sorting network for N keys is to first build a poset we call BOOL (N). Here we show some ideas on starting a sorting network for N keys when $N < 2^p$.

Fig. 13.8 Building
BOOL(16) [1]

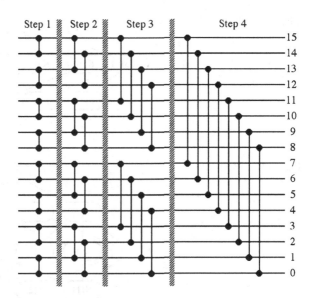

13.7.1 Removing Two Keys from BOOL(N)

Figure 13.8 is the Knuth diagram for building BOOL (16) in 4 steps.

Removing keys K[0] and K[15] will remove two comparators in each of the four steps: C(0, 1) and C(14, 15) in Step 1; C(0, 2) and C(13, 15) in Step 2; C(0, 4) and C(11, 15) in Step 3; and C(0, 8) and C(7, 15) in Step 4.

Note that keys K[1] and K[14] are not compared with any other keys in Step 1, keys K[2] and K[13] are not compared with any other keys in Step 2, keys K[4] and K[11] are not compared with any other keys in Step 3, and keys K[7] and K[8] are not compared with any other keys in Step 4. It makes sense to add C(1, 14) in Step 1, add C(2, 13) in Step 2, add C(4, 11) in Step 3 and add C(7, 8) in Step 4.

Figure 13.9 shows what this 14-key poset looks like.

It's useful to compare the 14-key poset with BOOL (16) shown in Fig. 13.10.

Keys K[0] and K[15] are removed and four coverings shown by dashed lines are added in Fig. 13.9. The added coverings insure that every key in the top rank are greater than every key in the bottom rank of Fig. 13.9. This eliminates all 0/1-cases where there is a High-0 in the top rank and a Low-1 in the bottom rank. We need not worry about these strangers that are so far out of place.

In general, for any BOOL (N) where $N \geq 8$, one can build a poset of $N-2$ keys by removing keys K[0] and K[N−1] and adding a comparator in each step to compare the two keys that are not compared with any other key in that step. The poset obtained will look like BOOL(N) except with keys K[0] and K[N−1] removed and p extra coverings added between the keys in the top rank and keys in the bottom rank. These extra coverings eliminate strangers that are far out of place.

Fig. 13.9 The 14-key Poset

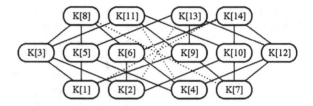

Fig. 13.10 BOOL(16)

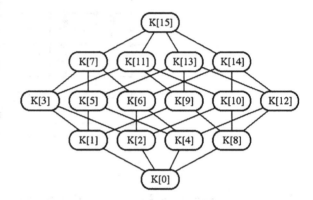

13.7.2 Removing Four Keys from BOOL (N)

The best way of starting out a sorting network for $N-4$ keys seems to use the rules in Sect. 13.7.1 to build two copies of a poset of $N/2-2$ keys and then to add a step comparing corresponding keys in the two posets.

13.7.3 Removing Eight Keys from BOOL (N)

The best way of starting out a sorting network for $N-8$ keys seems to use the rules in Sect. 13.7.2 to build two copies of a poset of $N/2-4$ keys and then to add a step comparing corresponding keys in the two posets.

References

1. Knuth D (1998) The art of computer programming. In: Sorting and searching, vol 3, 2nd edn. Addison-Wesley Longman, USA, pp 225–228
2. Edwards AWF (2002) Pascal's arithmetical triangle: the story of a mathematical idea. The Johns Hopkins University Press, Maryland

Chapter 14
Sorting Networks For Large N

Besides trying to find faster N-key sorting networks for $N \leq 32$, another goal can be trying and find a method for building fast sorting networks for $N > 32$. Here we assume that $N = 2^p$ for a large integer p so we can capitalize on our knowledge of BOOL(N).

14.1 Divide and Conquer

Let $S(N)$ be the number of steps required to sort N keys. Suppose we find a divide-and-conquer method that uses mp steps to reduce the problem of sorting N keys to sorting a number of groups in parallel where each group has no more than N^e keys where $e < 1$. If m and e are constants then the recursion for $S(N)$ is:

$$S(N) = mp + S(N^e) = m \log_2 N + S(N^e)$$

We define a function $f(p) = S(2^p)$ and substitute into the recursion to get:

$$f(p) = mp + f(pe)$$

which leads to:

$$f(p) = mp\left(1 + e + e^2 + e^3 + e^4 + \ldots\right) < mp/(1 - e).$$

or:

$$S(N) < mp/(1 - e) = m \log_2(N)/(1 - e)$$

We can sort 2^p keys in $mp/(1 - e)$ steps if we can find a divide-and-conquer method that has a small constant, m, and another constant, $e < 1$. As examples:

- if $e = 1/2$ then 2^p keys can be sorted in $2mp$ steps; or
- if $e = 2/3$ then 2^p keys can be sorted in $3mp$ steps.

S. W. Al-Haj Baddar and K. E. Batcher, *Designing Sorting Networks*,
DOI: 10.1007/978-1-4614-1851-1_14, © Springer Science+Business Media, LLC 2011

Fig. 14.1 $M(p)$ For Even p

p	$N = 2^p$	$M(p)$	$M(p)/N$	e so that $M(p) = N^e$
2	4	2	0.50000	0.50000
4	16	6	0.37500	0.64624
6	64	20	0.31250	0.72032
8	256	70	0.27344	0.76616
10	1024	252	0.24609	0.79773
12	4096	924	0.22559	0.82098
14	16384	3432	0.20947	0.83892
16	65536	12870	0.19638	0.85323
18	262144	48620	0.18547	0.86496
20	1048576	184756	0.17620	0.87476
22	4194304	705432	0.16819	0.88310
24	16777216	2704156	0.16118	0.89028
26	67108864	10400600	0.15498	0.89654
28	268435456	40116600	0.14945	0.90206
30	1073741824	155117520	0.14446	0.90696

14.2 The Middle Rank(s) of BOOL(N)

Let M(p) be the number of keys in the most highly populated rank(s) of BOOL(N). If p is even then rank-($p/2$) is the most highly populated rank. For even p from 2 to 30, Fig. 14.1 shows M(p), M(p)/N, and the value of e so that M(p) $= N^e$. If p is odd then rank-((p-1)/2) and rank-((p + 1)/2) are the most highly populated ranks. From Pascal's Triangle we see that if p is odd then M(p) $=$ M(p + 1)/2.

One can use Stirling's Approximation [1, 2] to show that M(p)/N is approximately $(2/(\text{pi}*p))^{0.5}$. M(p)/N does get smaller and smaller as p increases but the reduction is too slow. One can see this from the last column of Fig. 14.1, where the value of e so that M(p) $= N^e$ grows larger and larger toward unity as p increases.

At best, the p steps required to build BOOL(N) reduce the problem of sorting N keys to sorting M(p) keys but that's not enough of a reduction. Adding more steps after the p steps to build BOOL(N) will be useful if they simplify the problem of sorting N keys—if the number of additional steps is $O(p)$ we can still obtain an algorithm that sorts N keys in $O(p)$ steps.

14.3 Reducing The Number of Dimensions

The poset for BOOL(N) is a p-dimensional hypercube where each dimension has two values, 0 and 1. The N keys will be sorted only when they are arranged into a 1-dimensional chain so one can view the sorting problem as reducing the number of dimensions of the poset from p down to unity.

Fig. 14.2 BOOL(4)

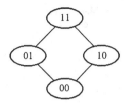

Fig. 14.3 Four keys sorted
in a chain (QUAD)

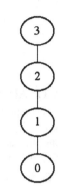

14.4 Combining Two Dimensions into One Dimension

BOOL(N) is the cardinal product, BOOL(4) * BOOL(N/4). It only takes one step
to sort the four keys in BOOL(4) (Fig. 14.2) into a chain which we call a **QUAD**
(Fig. 14.3).

To change BOOL(4) into QUAD, key **01** is compared with key **10**. Changing
BOOL(4) * BOOL(N/4) into QUAD * BOOL(N/4) requires one step with N/4
comparisons. Pick any two of the p dimensions in BOOL(N) and compare each
key in BOOL(N) where the bits in the two selected dimensions are **01** with the
corresponding key where the bits in the two selected dimensions are **10**. The N/4
comparisons are performed in parallel and only touch N/2 keys.

For example, let $N = 256$ and let each key be labeled with the eight-bit label
(**abcdefgh**). To change BOOL(256) into QUAD * BOOL(64) we pick dimensions
g and h and compare each key with label (**abcdef01**) with the corresponding key
with label (**abcdef10**). The 64 comparisons touch only 128 keys.

Another step of 64 comparisons will change QUAD * BOOL(64) into QUAD *
QUAD * BOOL(16). We pick dimensions e and f and compare each key with label
(**abcd01gh**) with the corresponding key with label (**abcd10gh**).

A third step of 64 comparisons will change QUAD * QUAD * BOOL(16) into
QUAD * QUAD * QUAD * BOOL(4). We pick dimensions c and d and compare
each key with label (**ab01efgh**) with the corresponding key with label (**ab10efgh**).

A fourth step of 64 comparisons will change QUAD * QUAD * QUAD *
BOOL(4) into QUAD * QUAD * QUAD * QUAD. We pick dimensions QUAD *

Fig. 14.4 Knuth diagram for
sorting eight keys

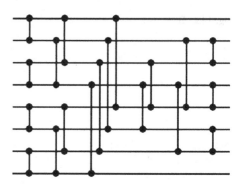

QUAD * QUAD * BOOL(4) and *b* and compare each key with label (**01cdefgh**) with the corresponding key with label (**10cdefgh**). The result is a poset with four dimensions with each dimension having four values: 0, 1, 2, 3.

In general, each step combines two of the *p* dimensions in BOOL(*N*) into a single dimension with four values. If *p* is even then *p*/2 steps will change the cardinal product of *p* BOOL(2) posets into the cardinal product of *p*/2 QUAD posets.

14.5 Combining Three Dimensions into One Dimensions

The Knuth diagram in Fig. 14.4 shows how eight keys can be sorted in six steps-the first three steps arrange the keys into a BOOL(8) and the last three steps convert the BOOL(8) into a chain of 8 keys which we call an OCTET.

Since BOOL(8) can be converted into an OCTET in three steps, we can convert BOOL(*N*) = BOOL(8) * BOOL(*N*/8) into OCTET * BOOL(*N*/8) in only three steps.

For example, let *N* = 256 and let each key be labeled with the eight-bit label (**abcdefgh**). To change BOOL(256) into OCTET * BOOL(32) we pick dimensions *f*, *g*, and *h* and use each comparison in the last three steps of Fig. 14.4 as a guide to each set of 32 comparisons in BOOL(256) as shown in Fig. 14.5.

14.6 Examples of Combining Dimensions

Here we show two examples, *N* = 16 and *N* = 32, to illustrate how combining dimensions simplifies sorting *N* keys.

16 KEYS: First we use four steps to form 16 keys into BOOL(16) and then two more steps to form QUAD * QUAD. The poset is shown in Fig. 14.6.

Fig. 14.5 Changing
BOOL(256) Into OCTET *
BOOL(32)

Step	Comparison in Fig. 14.4	32 comparisons in BOOL(256)
1	C(010,100)	(abcde010) with (abcde100)
	C(011,101)	(abcde011) with (abcde101)
2	C(001,100)	(abcde001) with (abcde100)
	C(011,110)	(abcde011) with (abcde110)
3	C(001,010)	(abcde001) with (abcde010)
	C(011,100)	(abcde011) with (abcde100)
	C(101,110)	(abcde101) with (abcde110)

Fig. 14.6 QUAD * QUAD

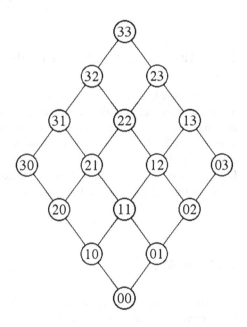

The QUAD * QUAD poset has seven ranks with four keys in the most populated rank. This is better than the five ranks of BOOL(16) with six keys in the
most populated rank. Also, the QUAD * QUAD poset has only 70 cases while
BOOL(16) has 168 cases.

32 KEYS: First we use five steps to form 32 keys into BOOL(32), then one more
step to form QUAD * BOOL(8), and then three more steps to form QUAD *
OCTET. The poset is shown in Fig. 14.7.

The QUAD * OCTET poset has eleven ranks with four keys in the most
populated ranks. This is better than the six ranks of BOOL(32) with ten keys in the
most populated ranks. Also, the QUAD * OCTET poset has only 495 cases while
BOOL(16) has 7,581 cases.

Fig. 14.7 QUAD * OCTET

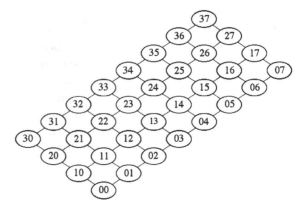

14.7 Minimizing Stranger Counts

After we use a number of steps to reduce the number of dimensions in the poset as much as possible, we pick a set of groups and use some number of steps to eliminate all strangers before we sort the groups. To minimize the number of strangers to be eliminated, we can add some merge steps after the groups are sorted. The larger the number of merge steps, the less the number of strangers. If each group contains 2^q keys then we can add q merge steps to merge the higher 2^{q-1} keys in each group with the lower 2^{q-1} keys in the next higher group. Note that $q < p$.

14.8 An Algorithm

Here we describe a promising algorithm for building a fast sorting network for a large number of keys. We assume that the number of keys, $N = 2^p$ for a large integer p and that $S(X)$ is the number of steps required to sort X keys. There is a number, $q(N)$, which still needs to be determined. There are three cases depending on the value of p mod 3:

- To sort $N = 2^p$ keys if p mod 3 = 0 use:

  1. *p steps to build BOOL(N)*;
  2. *p steps to convert BOOL(N) into the cardinal* product of *(p/3) OCTETS*;
  3. *$q(N)$ steps to eliminate all strangers*;
  4. *$S(N^{2/3})$ steps to sort $N^{1/3}$ groups of keys with $N^{2/3}$ keys in each group*; and
  5. *$(2p/3)$ steps to merge the highest $(N^{2/3}/2)$ keys in each group with the lowest $(N^{2/3}/2)$ keys in the next higher group.*

     This case uses $8p/3 + q(N) + S(N^{2/3})$ steps to sort N keys.

- To sort $N = 2^p$ keys if $p \bmod 3 = 1$ use:

  1. p steps to build BOOL(N);
  2. two steps to convert BOOL(N) into QUAD * QUAD * BOOL($N/16$)
  3. $(p-4)$ steps to convert QUAD * QUAD * BOOL($N/16$) into the cardinal product of two QUADS and $((p-4)/3)$ OCTETS;
  4. $q(N)$ steps to eliminate all strangers;
  5. $S((4\ N)^{2/3})$ steps to sort $(4\ N)^{1/3}/4$ groups of keys with $(4\ N)^{2/3}$ keys in each group; and
  6. $(2(p + 2)/3)$ steps to merge the highest $(4\ N)^{2/3}/2$ keys in each group with the lowest $(4\ N)^{2/3}/2$ keys in the next higher group.
  This case uses $(8p\text{-}2)/3 + q(N) + S((4\ N)^{2/3})$ steps to sort N keys

- To sort $N = 2^p$ keys if $p \bmod 3 = 2$ use:

  1. p steps to build BOOL(N);
  2. one step to convert BOOL(N) into QUAD * BOOL($N/4$)
  3. $(p-2)$ steps to convert QUAD * BOOL($N/4$) into the cardinal product of QUAD and $((p-2)/3)$ OCTETS;
  4. $q(N)$ steps to eliminate all strangers;
  5. $S((2\ N)^{2/3})$ steps to sort $(2\ N)^{1/3}/2$ groups of keys with $(2\ N)^{2/3}$ keys in each group; and
  6. $(2(p + 1)/3)$ steps to merge the highest $(2\ N)^{2/3}/2$ keys in each group with the lowest $(2\ N)^{2/3}/2$ keys in the next higher group.
  This case uses $(8p\text{-}1)/3 + q(N) + S((2\ N)^{2/3})$ steps to sort N keys.

If $q(N) = q(2^p)$ is $O(p)$ in all three cases then the algorithm will sort N keys in $O(p)$ steps.

References

1. Cormen T, Leiserson C, Rivest R, Stein C (2001) Introduction to algorithms, 2nd edn. McGraw-Hill Book Company, USA
2. Brassard G, Bratley P (1996) Fundamentals of algorithmics. Prentice Hall, New Jersey

Chapter 15
Another Way of Handling Strangers

Section 14.8 presents an algorithm for building sorting networks for large N. It mentions that we still need a method for eliminating all strangers after the dimension-reducing steps—here we suggest a way to do that.

After the dimension-reducing steps of the algorithm, the poset is a hypercube [1] (or hyper-rectangle) with less than p dimensions. Here we show a way of handling many of the strangers by considering the geometry of this poset.

Section 15.1 shows an example of eliminating many strangers from the QUAD * QUAD poset shown in Fig. 14.6; Sect. 15.2 shows an example of eliminating many strangers from the QUAD * OCTET poset shown in Fig. 14.7 and Sect. 15.3 describes the method in general.

15.1 Eliminating Strangers in the QUAD * QUAD Poset

Figure 15.1 is a copy of the 4 × 4 diagram for the QUAD * QUAD poset.

- If key 23 has a High-0 then all keys in the 3 × 4 rectangle below it must also be zeroes so the 0/1-case must have at least 12 zeroes. The case can have at most 4 ones and these ones can only be in keys 30, 31, 32, or 33. To eliminate the High-0 in key 23 we can compare it with key 30, 31, or 32 (key 33 is > key 23 so we exclude it as a possible match.) Any ones in keys 30, 31, and 32 are sorted toward key 32 so the best place to find a one to compare with the High-0 in key 23 is in key 32.
- Similarly, if key 32 has a High-0 the best place to find a one to compare with it is in key 23. Comparing key 23 with key 32 will eliminate a High-0 in either of the two keys.
- If key 13 has a High-0 then all keys in the 2 × 4 rectangle below it must also be zeroes so the 0/1-case must have at least 8 zeroes and any ones in that case must be in the 2 × 4 rectangle ≥ key 20. These ones will be sorted toward the top. We've already decided to compare keys 32 and 23, so the best choice is key 22 or key 31. We decide to compare key 13 with 31 because that also eliminates any High-0 in key 31.

S. W. Al-Haj Baddar and K. E. Batcher, *Designing Sorting Networks*,
DOI: 10.1007/978-1-4614-1851-1_15, © Springer Science+Business Media, LLC 2011

Fig. 15.1 QUAD * QUAD

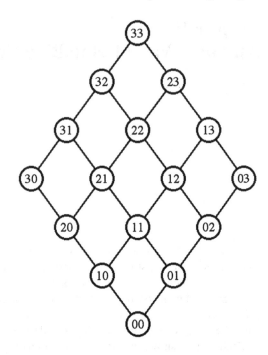

Fig. 15.2 Matching
strangers in QUAD * QUAD

Key	Number of Keys		Matching Key
	≤ Key	≥ Key	
23	12	2	32
32	12	2	23
22	9	4	30
13	8	3	31
31	8	3	13
12	6	6	21
21	6	6	12
03	4	4	11
30	4	4	22
11	4	9	03
02	3	8	20
20	3	8	02
01	2	12	10
10	2	12	01

- If key 22 has a High-0 then all keys in the 3 × 3 rectangle below it must also be zeroes so the 0/1-case must have at least 9 zeroes. Any ones in this case can only be in keys 03, 13, 23, 30, 31, 32, and 33. The only keys in this set that are available for comparison are keys 03 or 30. We pick 30 arbitrarily.

Fig. 15.3 QUAD * QUAD after strangers are matched

k	Number of Keys		Keys covering k	Keys covered by k
	> k	< k		
0	15	0	1	
1	14	1	2 3 4	0
2	11	2	5 6 8 10	1
4	10	2	5 6 8	1
3	9	2	5 6	1
6	7	5	7 9	2 3 4
8	6	4	9	2 4
10	5	3	11 12 13	2
5	3	5	13	2 3 4
7	4	6	11 13	6
9	5	7	11 12 13	6 8
12	2	9	14	9 10
11	2	10	14	7 9 10
13	2	11	14	5 7 9 10
14	1	14	15	11 12 13
15	0	15		14

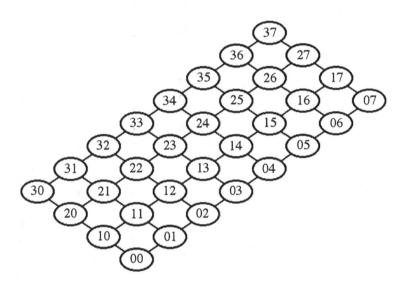

Fig. 15.4 QUAD * OCTET

- By duality, the best way to eliminate Low-1's at the bottom of the diagram is to compare key 01 with key 10, key 02 with key 20, and key 11 with key 03.
- The only keys that are still available for comparisons are keys 12 and 21 so we compare one with the other.

Figure 15.2 shows a table of these comparisons in the QUAD * QUAD poset. Comparing these strangers with their matching keys reduces the number of 0/1-cases from 70 to 50 and generates the poset depicted in Fig. 15.3.

Key	Number of Keys		Matching Key
	≤ Key	≥ Key	
36	28	2	27
27	24	2	36
35	24	3	26
26	21	4	35
34	20	4	25
25	18	6	34
17	16	3	33
33	16	5	17
24	15	8	16
16	14	6	24
32	12	6	15
15	12	9	32
23	12	10	07
07	8	4	23
31	8	7	06
06	7	8	31
30	4	8	14
14	10	12	30
22	9	12	05
05	6	12	22
21	6	14	13
13	8	15	21
04	5	16	20
20	3	16	04
12	6	18	03
03	4	20	12
11	4	21	02
02	3	24	11
10	2	24	01
01	2	28	10

15.2 Eliminating Strangers in the QUAD * OCTET Poset

Figure 15.4 is a copy of the 4 × 8 diagram for the QUAD * OCTET poset.

In a manner similar to the QUAD * QUAD poset we examine the diagram geometrically to find the best matches for the High-0's and Low-1's. Figure 15.5 shows the table of matches that were obtained.

15.3 The Method in General

The examples in Sects. 15.1 and 15.2 illustrate the method. After reducing the number of dimensions, examine the hypercube (or hyper-rectangle) geometrically to determine the best matches for High-0's and Low-1's. If the number of keys is very large a spreadsheet like Excel might be useful.

Reference

1. Rosen K (2003) Discrete mathematics and its applications, 5th edn. McGraw-Hill Companies, Aurora

Chapter 16
Thoughts on Minimizing Strangers

Here are some thoughts about minimizing strangers in an N-key network.

16.1 Minimizing Strangers

Definitions For each key, x, we define:

- $GE(x)$ to be the set of keys that are greater than or equal to x in the poset;
- $LE(x)$ to be the set of keys that are less than or equal to x in the poset;
- $N0(x)$ to be the number of 0-entries in row-x of the Shmoo Chart;
- $N1(x)$ to be the number of 1-entries in row-x of the Shmoo Chart; and
- $NS(x)$ to be the number of strangers in row-x of the Shmoo Chart so $NS(x) = N + 1 - N0(x) - N1(x)$.

00000 . . . 00000	----- . . . -----	11111 . . . 11111
$N0(x)$	$NS(x)$	$N1(x)$

Relations Between N0(X), N1(X), GE(X), and LE(X)
Let $|GE(x)|$ be the number of keys in $GE(x)$ and let $|LE(x)|$ be the number of keys in $LE(x)$. How are $N0(x)$ and $N1(x)$ related to $|GE(x)|$ and $|LE(x)|$?

The leftmost 1-entry in row-x of the Shmoo Chart is in the column of all cases with exactly $(N1(x)-1)$ zeroes. Why do none of these cases have a 0-value in key-x? Because if any of these cases did have a 0-value in key-x then that case would also need to have a 0-value in every key in $LE(x)$. There aren't enough zeroes in these cases; i.e.,

$$(N1(x) - 1) < |LE(x)|.$$

S. W. Al-Haj Baddar and K. E. Batcher, *Designing Sorting Networks*,
DOI: 10.1007/978-1-4614-1851-1_16, © Springer Science+Business Media, LLC 2011

But when we move left one column in the Shmoo Chart to the column of cases with $N1(x)$ zeroes we find that there are some of these cases which do have a 0-value in key-x so:

$$N1(x) = |LE(x)|.$$

By duality[1] we also have:

$$N0(x) = |GE(x)|.$$

Comparing Key-x With Key-y

What happens when the next step in the network contains a comparator that compares key-x with key-y to put their maximum value in key-max(x,y) and their minimum value in key-min(x,y)? If $\vee$ denotes the set-union operation then:

1. $N0(\max(x,y)) = \min(N0(x), N0(y)) = \min(|GE(x)|, |GE(y)|)$;
2. $N1(\max(x,y)) = |LE(x) \vee LE(y)|$;
3. $N0(\min(x,y)) = |GE(x) \vee GE(y)|$; and
4. $N1(\min(x,y)) = \min(N1(x), N1(y)) = \min(|LE(x)|, |LE(y)|)$.

To minimize the number of strangers in key-max(x,y) and key-min(x,y) one should pick a comparator that maximizes the sum of 1, 2, 3, and 4.

Let $W(x,y)$ be the *worth* of a comparator that compares key-x with key-y; i.e., the number of strangers that that comparator eliminates. Before the comparator there are:

- $N + 1 - N0(x) - N1(x)$ strangers in key-x and
- $N + 1 - N0(y) - N1(y)$ strangers in key-y.

After the comparator there are:

- $N + 1 - N0(\max(x,y)) - N1(\max(x,y))$ strangers in key-max(x,y) and
- $N + 1 - N0(\min(x,y)) - N1(\min(x,y))$ strangers in key-min(x,y).

So:

$$
\begin{aligned}
W(x, y) &= N0(\max(x,y)) + N1(\max(x,y)) + N0(\min(x,y)) + N1(\min(x,y)) \\
&\quad - N0(x) - N1(x) - N0(y) - N1(y). \\
&= LE(x) \vee LE(y)|+|GE(x) \vee GE(y)|+\min(|GE(x)|, |GE(y)|) + \min(|LE(x)|, \\
&\quad |LE(y)|) - |GE(x)| - |LE(x)| - |GE(y)| - |LE(y)|. \\
&= |LE(x) \vee LE(y)| - \max(|LE(x)|, |LE(y)|) + |GE(x) \vee GE(y)| - \max(|GE(x)|, \\
&\quad |GE(y)|).
\end{aligned}
$$

SHOW.WORTHS

A new command, **SHOW.WORTHS**, was added Sortnet. **SHOW.WORTHS** displays an N-column by N-row array. The entry in column-x and row-y of the array shows the worth of comparing key-x with key-y.

A strategy to minimize strangers

To minimize strangers as much as possible select the comparators that have the largest entries in the **SHOW.WORTHS** display.

- It's easier if the goal is to design an efficient sorting network (a network with the least number of comparators.) Pick a comparator with the largest worth, add it to the comparator list, and then **GEN.CASES** and **SHOW.WORTHS** to pick the next comparator.
- It's harder if the goal is to design a fast sorting network (a network with the least number of steps.) Pick a set of comparators with no two comparators sharing the same keys that maximizes the sum of all comparator worths.

16.2 Minimizing Strangers & Preserving Orderings

Here are some more thoughts about minimizing strangers in an N-key network while preserving partial-orderings.

Preserving Partial Orderings

Recall Sect. 3.1- if one is not careful then a comparator in some step might destroy some of the partial-orderings that were established in earlier steps.

To minimize strangers, suppose one adds a comparator in some step to compare key-x with key-y. Theorem 3-1 in Chap. 3 says that to preserve partial-orderings, one should also add other comparators to the step:

- to compare keys in GE(x) with corresponding keys in GE(y); and
- to compare keys in LE(x) with corresponding keys in LE(y).

In the previous section we learned that the best way to minimize strangers was to maximize |GE(x) $\lor$ GE(y)| and |LE(x) $\lor$ LE(y)| by minimizing |GE(x) $\land$ GE(y)| and |LE(x) $\land$ LE(y)| where $\land$ denotes the set-intersection operator. Minimizing the number of keys in the intersections will also make the additional comparisons good at minimizing strangers.

Example Figure 16.1 shows the Shmoo chart for BOOL(32). Suppose a comparator compares key-19 (10011) with key-28 (11100). Fig. 16.2 shows the poset of the keys that are in GE(10011), GE(11100), LE(10011), and LE(11100).

To preserve as many orderings as possible the following seven comparators should also be added:

- Key-23 (10111) with key-29 (11101);
- Key-27 (11011) with key-30 (11110);
- Key-3 (00011) with key-12 (01100);
- Key-18 (10010) with key-20 (10100);
- Key-17 (10001) with key-24 (11000);
- Key-2 (00010) with key-4 (00100); and
- Key-1 (00001) with key-8 (01000).

```
     Number of Zeroes in Case
     33322222222222211111111111 0000000000        No. of Cases     No. of Dashes
     21098765432109876543210987 6543210           where key = 1
 31: 0111111111111111111111111111111 :                7580              0
 30: 00--------------1111111111111111 :               7413             15
 29: 00--------------1111111111111111 :               7413             15
 27: 00--------------1111111111111111 :               7413             15
 23: 00--------------1111111111111111 :               7413             15
 15: 00--------------1111111111111111 :               7413             15
 28: 0000--------------------11111111 :               5573             21
 26: 0000--------------------11111111 :               5573             21
 25: 0000--------------------11111111 :               5573             21
 22: 0000--------------------11111111 :               5573             21
 21: 0000--------------------11111111 :               5573             21
 19: 0000--------------------11111111 :               5573             21
 14: 0000--------------------11111111 :               5573             21
 13: 0000--------------------11111111 :               5573             21
 11: 0000--------------------11111111 :               5573             21
  7: 0000--------------------11111111 :               5573             21
 24: 00000000--------------------1111 :               2008             21
 20: 00000000--------------------1111 :               2008             21
 18: 00000000--------------------1111 :               2008             21
 17: 00000000--------------------1111 :               2008             21
 12: 00000000--------------------1111 :               2008             21
 10: 00000000--------------------1111 :               2008             21
  9: 00000000--------------------1111 :               2008             21
  6: 00000000--------------------1111 :               2008             21
  5: 00000000--------------------1111 :               2008             21
  3: 00000000--------------------1111 :               2008             21
 16: 0000000000000000--------------11 :                168             15
  8: 0000000000000000--------------11 :                168             15
  4: 0000000000000000--------------11 :                168             15
  2: 0000000000000000--------------11 :                168             15
  1: 0000000000000000--------------11 :                168             15
  0: 00000000000000000000000000000001 :                  1              0
```

Fig. 16.1 Shmoo chart for bool(32)

Fig. 16.2 GE(10011), GE(11100), LE(10011), and LE(11100)

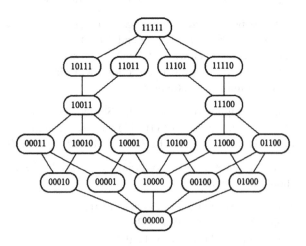

```
       Number of Zeroes in Case
       33322222222222111111111110000000000     No. of Cases        No. of Dashes
       21098765432109876543210987654321 0      where key = 1
 31: 01111111111111111111111111111111 :          6113                 0
 30: 00-------1111111111111111111111111 :         6096                 7
 29: 00-------1111111111111111111111111 :         6096                 7
 15: 00--------------1111111111111111 :           5964                15
 27: 000------------1111111111111111 :            5823                14
 23: 000------------1111111111111111 :            5823                14
 14: 0000--------------------11111111 :           4304                21
 13: 0000--------------------11111111 :           4304                21
 11: 0000--------------------11111111 :           4304                21
  7: 0000--------------------11111111 :           4304                21
 25: 0000--------------------11111111 :           4270                21
 22: 0000--------------------11111111 :           4270                21
 26: 0000--------------------11111111 :           4195                21
 21: 0000--------------------11111111 :           4195                21
 28: 0000--------------------11111111 :           4142                21
 19: 0000--------------------11111111 :           4142                21
 12: 00000000----------------1111111 :            2293                18
 24: 00000000-----------------111111 :            2088                19
 20: 00000000-----------------111111 :            2088                19
  9: 00000000--------------------1111 :           1434                21
  6: 00000000--------------------1111 :           1434                21
 10: 00000000--------------------1111 :           1397                21
  5: 00000000--------------------1111 :           1397                21
 18: 000000000000----------------1111 :            596                17
 17: 000000000000----------------1111 :            596                17
  3: 00000000000000--------------1111 :            481                15
  8: 0000000000000000-----------111 :             220                14
  4: 0000000000000000-----------111 :             220                14
 16: 0000000000000000--------------11 :            138                15
  2: 00000000000000000000000-------11 :             15                 7
  1: 00000000000000000000000-------11 :             15                 7
  0: 00000000000000000000000000000001 :              1                 0
```

Fig. 16.3 Shmoo chart after the 8 comparators

These eight comparators give us the Shmoo chart in Fig. 16.3

Seven more comparators could be added in the same step. What's the best choice for these comparators?

Reference

1. Rosen K (2003) Discrete mathematics and its applications, 5th edn. McGraw-Hill Companies, USA

Chapter 17
Case Studies

Here we describe a heuristic technique for designing faster sorting networks. This technique helped design an 18-key and a 22-key sorting networks that are faster than the corresponding merge-sorting networks [1]. These two networks were designed using Sortnet and they will also be described in this chapter.

17.1 A Heuristic Technique for Designing Faster Sorting Networks

Experimentation with Sortnet helped develop a heuristic technique for designing faster sorting networks that comprises three stages: finding a good single-segment poset, generating a stair-case Shmoo chart, and finalizing the sorting. Here we describe these stages.

17.1.1 Finding a Good Single-Segment Poset

If you examine any sorting network, you will notice that the first few steps are spent on forming a single-segment poset. Before sorting, each key constitutes a segment in the initial N-segment poset. In the next step, each two keys get compared resulting in an $N/2$ segment poset. This continues until you form the single-segment poset. This raises many questions like: how many steps do you spend designing the single-segment poset? is there a unified way(an algorithm for instance) to form single-segment posets? and how can we measure the goodness of a single-segment poset?

If you study the fastest sorting networks, especially those with input sizes that are powers of two, you will notice that they preserve as much information as possible while forming the single-segment poset. Chapter 3 illustrated how to

S. W. Al-Haj Baddar and K. E. Batcher, *Designing Sorting Networks*,
DOI: 10.1007/978-1-4614-1851-1_17, © Springer Science+Business Media, LLC 2011

connect the corresponding keys so as to preserve as much information as possible and this applies smoothly to power-of-two input sizes. However, we aimed, in the case studies described here, at finding the best way to create a single-segment poset for even input sizes that are not powers of 2. The problem, here, is that there is no straight forward way to create these posets for such input sizes. Consider for instance designing a single-segment poset for 22 keys. You can get your single-segment poset by combining two 11-key posets together, and let us call this option I. Another option would be connecting one 10-key poset with one 12-key poset. A third option, option III, would be to connect two 8-key segment posets with one 6-key segment poset. All of these options will result in a single-segment poset of 22 keys. The question is which option is the best? Also for options II and III, there are many ways to connect the keys to form the poset. Thus, which of these possible ways is better for generating a single-segment poset that preserves as much information as possible and helps find a faster sorting network?

So far, there is no definite answer to these questions. Thus, heuristic answers are sought and the significance of using Sortnet appears here. The experimentations that were conducted using Sortnet showed that single-segment posets with relatively smaller number of 0/1-cases usually help design faster sorting networks. Sortnet can provide the network designer with the corresponding number of 0/1-cases generated by each single-segment poset. Thus, the user plugs in the comparators to implement either option I, any form of option II, or any form of option III and saves the number of cases generated by each possible single-segment poset. Then, the user can select the single-segment poset with the fewest number of 0/1-cases.

17.1.2 Obtaining the Staircase-Shaped Shmoo Chart

An N-key single-segment poset where N is an even non-power-of-two integer is usually hard to work with. Thus, examining the poset at this stage will not help select the comparators to use in the subsequent steps. Now, the question is what should the designer do? An end-game approach can provide a heuristic for selecting the best comparators to use. If you examine the Shmoo charts of the final steps in the fastest sorting networks, you will notice that they all exhibit a uniform staircase pattern. Thus, the designer can set a goal at this stage, which is to reach a staircase Shmoo chart pattern using the fewest possible number of steps.

What is the best way to generate this Shmoo chart? Again, there is no definite answer to this question. But, a Sortnet command, **SHOW.BESTCE**, proved to be useful. As mention in Chap. 6, this command displays the comparators that remove the most dashes and/or affect the most cases together with the earliest step in which they can be plugged. Thus, the user can select from these comparators and add them to the network. After that, the designer can use the Sortnet command **SHOW.SHMOO** to display the Shmoo chart and see what it looks like after applying these comparators.

If the network designer plugs in the comparators that appear in the lowest lines of the **SHOW.BESTCE** display, then they will remove more dashes. Alternatively, if they select the comparators that appear in the upper lines of the **SHOW.BESTCE** display, then they will affect more cases. The designer can either focus on removing more dashes or affecting more cases for consecutive steps or can alternate between these two strategies. Obviously, the designer can backtrack to earlier steps, using the **CUT.CE.STEPS** command, and select a different strategy for picking comparators until the designated Shmoo chart is obtained using the desired number of steps.

A different strategy that one may want to try is to pick the comparators based on the keys' relative positions in the Shmoo chart. For example, comparing the keys that appear next to each other in the Shmoo chart usually helps eliminate more cases (see Chap. 12).

These different heuristics may sound confusing. However, experimentation showed that if the designer succeeds in designing a good single-segment poset that preserve information, then a Shmoo chart with the desired staircase pattern would be reached relatively easily. So, the different strategies applied by the user will lead to the designated Shmoo chart within a relatively small number of steps.

17.1.3 Finalizing the Sorting

After generating a Shmoo chart with the staircase pattern, the subsequent steps become straight forward. All the designer has to do is to compare each two adjacent keys in the Shmoo chart and generate the corresponding new Shmoo chart. This, process will be repeated until a dash-free Shmoo chart is obtained within the desired number of steps.

17.1.4 The Number of Steps

A reasonable question is how to determine the number of steps for each of the network design stages (forming the single-segment poset, finding the staircase Shmoo chart, and finalizing the sorting)? Assume that you want to sort the N keys of a sorting network in p steps. It is typical to spend nearly log N steps in the single-segment formation step. This leaves out $q = p - $ Log N steps. Experimentation showed that for $N \leq 32$, no more than 50% of the q steps is spent in the third stage [1]. Thus, if you choose the desired number of steps p ahead of time, then it will help you roughly estimate how many steps you want to spend in each stage.

The experimentations showed that the better the single-segment is the smoother it will be to find the staircase Shmoo chart within the desired number of steps. If you find yourself struggling in the second stage of the network design and not reaching the staircase Shmoo chart within the number of steps you planned on, then maybe you need to give your single-segment poset a second thought. A good single-segment poset will automatically help you in the second stage despite the strategy you choose; i.e., concentrating on removing dashes, concentrating on affecting more cases or comparing adjacent keys in the Shmoo chart.

It is worth mentioning that using this technique for designing sorting networks facilitated discovering promising networks including: 20-key, 24-key, and 26-key sorting networks. For each of these three input sizes, a network that is as fast at the merge-sorting network but with fewer CEs in the last step have been already found. Currently, more experimentation is being done in order to beat the merge-sorting number of steps for these input sizes.

The experimentation on even non-power-of-two input sizes might not be practically appealing. However, this work aimed at proving that the gap in the number of steps between the theoretic lower bound and the fastest merge-sorting networks is reducible (see Chap. 9).

17.2 An 11-Step Network for Sorting 18 Keys

Here we will briefly describe the 11-step network, for sorting 18 keys [2] that is one step faster than Batcher's 18-key merge-sorting network. The technique described in Sect. 17.1 helped design this network. Figure 17.1 illustrates this network.

17.2.1 Designing the Single-segment Poset in Steps 1 Through 4

As described in Sect. 17.1, there are several ways to design a single-segment poset comprising 18 keys. One can try to build two 9-key posets and then connect the corresponding keys from each poset. However, you might not prefer this alternative since it implies handling posets with odd number of keys (see Chap. 9). An alternative would be a three-segment poset where each segment is a honeycomb of 6 keys. This option looks more appealing than the two 9-key posets. However, experimentation with it did not lead to the staircase Shmoo chart within the desired number of steps. Thus, a third option, namely a two-segment poset with one segment having 8 keys and the other having 10 keys, was considered and it worked. Of course, this does not prove that this is the only way to find a faster sorting network for 18 keys. It only proves it is a smoother option to work with because using it helped obtain the desired Shmoo chart relatively easily. Besides, the number of 0/1-cases generated using this option was relatively smaller than the corresponding numbers generated by the two other options [1].

It takes three steps to form a two-segment poset. In the fourth step, the keys in the two posets need to be connected to form a single-segment poset. Again, different alternatives do exist. Several ways for connecting the two posets were

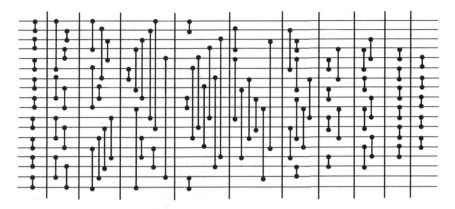

Fig. 17.1 The Knuth diagram of the 11-step network for sorting 18 keys [2]

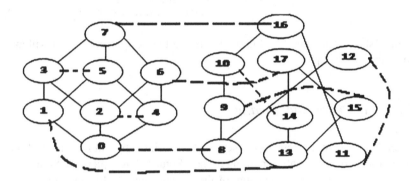

Fig. 17.2 The single-segment poset obtained after applying step 4

tested. But, the one in Fig. 17.2 helped preserve more information and led to a smoother second stage.

17.2.2 Obtaining the Staircase Shmoo Chart

Five steps were spent in the second stage of sorting (i.e., obtaining the staircase Shmoo chart) and 2 steps in finalizing the network. Affecting the most cases was targeted in step 5. In steps 6 and 7, removing as many dashes as possible from the Shmoo chart was sought. Removing dashes was used again in steps 8 and 9 and resulted in the Shmoo chart depicted in Fig. 17.3. Obviously, this Shmoo chart exhibits the staircase pattern described in Sect. 17.1.

It is worth mentioning that the strategy used in this network is not the only one that leads to the staircase pattern depicted in Fig. 17.3. Other possible strategies

Fig. 17.3 The Shmoo chart
after step 9 [1]

```
Number of Zeroes in Case
1111111110000000000    No. of Cases
8765432109876543210    where key = 1

17: 0111111111111111111 :              38
16: 0011111111111111111 :              37
15: 0001111111111111111 :              36
14: 0000--1111111111111 :              33
13: 0000--1111111111111 :              32
11: 00000---11111111111 :              29
12: 00000---11111111111 :              27
 9: 0000000---111111111 :              23
10: 0000000---111111111 :              22
 8: 000000000---1111111 :              17
 7: 000000000---1111111 :              16
 5: 00000000000---11111 :              12
 6: 00000000000---11111 :              10
 4: 0000000000000--1111 :               7
 3: 0000000000000--1111 :               6
 2: 0000000000000000111 :               3
 1: 0000000000000000011 :               2
 0: 0000000000000000001 :               1
```

for these steps were tested and they also led to the designated pattern within the
same number of steps.

17.2.3 Finalizing the Sorting

The tenth and eleventh steps were spent on comparing adjacent keys in the Shmoo
chart in order to remove all remaining dashes. Figure 17.4 depicts the Shmoo chart
obtained after applying the last step of the network depicted in Fig. 17.1.

Note that that by designing this network, faster networks for some other values
of N can be easily obtained. For Example, a 36-key sorting network that utilizes two
18-key sorting networks then merges them can now be designed using the faster 18-
key network. As a consequence, we obtain a 17-step 36-key network instead of the
previous 18-step 36-key sorting network. Moreover, a faster 17-key sorting network
is now achievable since such a network removes a key form the fastest 18-key
network in order to sort the 17 keys. Now, this 17-key network requires only 11
steps instead of 12. All networks with sizes that are multiples of 18 or 17 can utilize
this 11-step 18-key network to design faster sorting networks.

17.3 A 12-Step Network for Sorting 22 Keys

In this section, we describe a 12-step 22-key network that is one step faster than
Batcher's merge sorting 13-step network for 22-keys [1]. Figure 17.5 depicts the
Knuth diagram of this network. Again, the technique described in Sect. 17.1 was
used to help design this network.

Fig. 17.4 The Shmoo chart
after step 11 [1]

```
              Number of Zeroes in Case
              1111111110000000000    No. of Cases
              8765432109876543210    where key = 1

         17:  0111111111111111111 :        18
         16:  0011111111111111111 :        17
         15:  0001111111111111111 :        16
         14:  0000111111111111111 :        15
         13:  0000011111111111111 :        14
         12:  0000001111111111111 :        13
         11:  0000000111111111111 :        12
         10:  0000000011111111111 :        11
          9:  0000000001111111111 :        10
          8:  0000000000111111111 :         9
          7:  0000000000011111111 :         8
          6:  0000000000001111111 :         7
          5:  0000000000000111111 :         6
          4:  0000000000000011111 :         5
          3:  0000000000000001111 :         4
          2:  0000000000000000111 :         3
          1:  0000000000000000011 :         2
          0:  0000000000000000001 :         1
```

17.3.1 Designing the Single-Segment Poset in Steps 1 Through 4

The first three steps were spent on designing a multi-segment 22-key poset. For 22 keys, there are several possible ways to construct such a poset as described in Sect. 17.1. Which of these ways is the best? Sortnet helped answer this question by providing the number of 0/1-cases that resulted from each possible poset. Consequently, a three-segment poset comprising one 6-key poset and two 8-key posets, was selected.

The fourth step has to connect the keys in the three-segment poset in such a way that preserves information as much as possible. Several ways exist to do so. But, which one of them is the best? Sortnet, helped find the comparators described in Fig. 17.6. Of course, we do not claim that this poset is the best possible poset or the most information preserving poset for 22 keys. However, it simply helped going through the second stage of sorting and obtain the desired Shmoo chart within the predetermined number of steps.

17.3.2 Obtaining the Staircase Shmoo Chart

In order to obtain the staircase Shmoo chart 5 steps were spent in this stage. In steps 5 and 6 the comparators that removed the most dashes were selected whereas

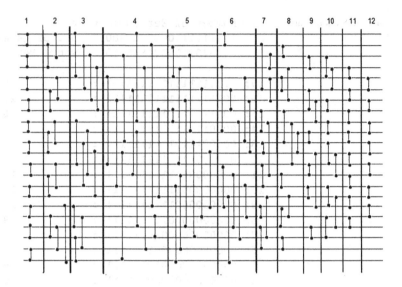

Fig. 17.5 The Knuth diagram of the 12-step network for sorting 22 keys [1]

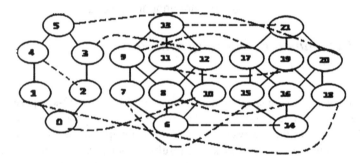

Fig. 17.6 The single-segment poset obtained after applying step 4 of the network in Fig. 17.5

the comparators that affected the most cases were used in step 7. In steps 8 and 9, the comparators that removed the most dashes were also selected and the resulting Shmoo chart is depicted in Fig. 17.7. Obviously, this Shmoo chart exhibits the desired staircase pattern sought in this stage of design.

17.3.3 Finalizing the Sorting

In the three remaining steps, the keys that are adjacent in the Shmoo chart were compared in order to reach the dash-free Shmoo chart. Figure 17.8 depicts the dash-free Shmoo chart obtained after plugging the comparators of the last 3 steps.

Fig. 17.7 The Shmoo chart
after step 9 [1]

```
            Number of Zeroes in Case
            2221111111111000000000      No. of Cases
            2109876543210987654321      where key = 1

        21: 011111111111111111111111 :        73
        20: 001111111111111111111111 :        72
        17: 000--11111111111111111111 :        69
        19: 000---1111111111111111111 :        68
        16: 0000----111111111111111111 :       64
        18: 0000----111111111111111111 :       61
        15: 000000----1111111111111111 :       56
        14: 00000-----1111111111111111 :       55
        12: 0000000-----11111111111111 :       48
        13: 0000000-----11111111111111 :       44
         9: 000000000-----111111111111 :       39
        11: 000000000------111111111111 :      35
        10: 00000000000-----1111111111 :       30
         8: 00000000000-----1111111111 :       26
         7: 0000000000000-----11111111 :       19
         5: 0000000000000----111111111 :       18
         3: 000000000000000----11111111 :      13
         6: 000000000000000----11111111 :      10
         2: 00000000000000000---111111 :        6
         4: 000000000000000000--111111 :        5
         1: 000000000000000000000011 :        2
         0: 000000000000000000000001 :        1
```

Fig. 17.8 The 22-key
dash-free Shmoo chart after
step 12 [1]

```
            Number of Zeroes in Case
            2221111111111000000000      No. of Cases
            2109876543210987654321      where key = 1

        21: 011111111111111111111111 :        22
        20: 001111111111111111111111 :        21
        19: 000111111111111111111111 :        20
        18: 000011111111111111111111 :        19
        17: 000001111111111111111111 :        18
        16: 000000111111111111111111 :        17
        15: 000000011111111111111111 :        16
        14: 000000001111111111111111 :        15
        13: 000000000111111111111111 :        14
        12: 000000000011111111111111 :        13
        11: 000000000001111111111111 :        12
        10: 000000000000111111111111 :        11
         9: 000000000000011111111111 :        10
         8: 000000000000001111111111 :         9
         7: 000000000000000111111111 :         8
         6: 000000000000000011111111 :         7
         5: 000000000000000001111111 :         6
         4: 000000000000000000111111 :         5
         3: 000000000000000000011111 :         4
         2: 000000000000000000001111 :         3
         1: 000000000000000000000011 :         2
         0: 000000000000000000000001 :         1
```

As mentioned in Sect. 17.2, a by-product of designing this network is faster
networks for networks with input sizes that are multiples of either 22 or 21
keys.

References

1. Al-Haj Baddar S, Batcher KE (2009) Finding faster sorting networks using sortnet. VDM Publishing House Ltd, Germany
2. Al-Haj Baddar S, Batcher KE (2009) An 11-step sorting network for 18 elements. Parallel Process Lett 19(1):97–104

Appendix I
Proofs of Theorems

Theorem 1.1 *If $A = \{a_1, a_2, \ldots, a_{2N-1}, a_{2N}\}$ is any bitonic sequence with 2N keys, and if*

$$H = \{\max(a_1, a_{N+1}), \max(a_2, a_{N+2}), \ldots, \max(a_N, a_{2N})\},$$

and if

$$L = \{\min(a_1, a_{N+1}), \min(a_2, a_{N+2}), \ldots, \min(a_N, a_{2N})\},$$

then:

1. *the H-sequence is a bitonic sequence of N keys;*
2. *the L-sequence is another bitonic sequence of the other N keys; and*
3. *every key in the H-sequence is greater than or equal to every key in the L-sequence (so the H-sequence contains the greatest N keys of A and the L-sequence contains the least N keys of A).*

Proof Place the 2N keys of A equally-spaced around the circumference of a circle as shown in Fig. I.1–note that each of the keys in the H and L sequences is found by comparing elements that are diametrically-opposite on this circle.

Let a_H have the maximum value of all keys in A and let a_L have the minimum value. They can appear anywhere on the circle as shown in Fig. I.2–note that since A is bitonic, an ascending (non-decreasing) sequence of keys is traversed in going from a_L to a_H whether the traversal is in the clockwise direction or in the counter-clockwise direction.

Let $a_{H'}$ be the key that is diametrically-opposite to a_H and let $a_{L'}$ be the key that is diametrically-opposite to a_L as shown in Fig. I.3. Let T be the traversal from a_L to a_H that traverses the least number of keys and let T' be the traversal diametrically opposite from T going from $a_{L'}$ to $a_{H'}$. Note that T traverses an ascending (non-decreasing) sequence of keys while T' traverses a descending (non-increasing) sequence of keys.

S. W. Al-Haj Baddar and K. E. Batcher, *Designing Sorting Networks*,
DOI: 10.1007/978-1-4614-1851-1, © Springer Science+Business Media, LLC 2011

Fig. I.1

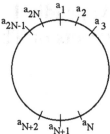

Fig. I.2

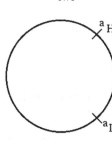

Fig. I.3

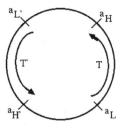

Fig. I.4

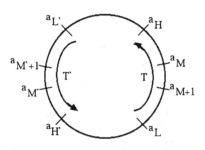

But $a_H \geq a_{H'}$ because a_H has the maximum value of all keys. Similarly, $a_L \leq a_{L'}$ because a_L has the minimum value of all keys. This means that somewhere along T there is a key a_M where $a_M \geq a_{M'}$ and $a_{M+1} \leq a_{M'+1}$ as shown in Fig. I.4.

Let X be the traversal starting at $a_{M'+1}$, going through $a_{L'}$ and a_H, and ending at a_M (as shown in Fig. I.5) and let Y be the traversal diametrically opposite of X starting at a_{M+1}, going through a_L and $a_{H'}$, and ending at $a_{M'}$.

Note that X increases up to a_H and then decreases and that Y decreases down to a_L and then increases. Both X and Y are bitonic sequences.

Fig. I.5

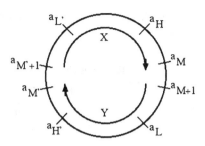

Note that each element of X is greater than or equal to every element of Y so $X = H$ with some cyclic rotation and $Y = L$ with some cyclic rotation and the theorem is proven. This proof can be simplified using the 0/1-principle introduced in Chap. 4.

Theorem 1.2 *Let* $A = \{a_1, a_2, ..., a_{m-1}, a_m\}$ *be a sequence of m keys; let* $B = f\{b_1, b_2, ..., b_{n-1}, b_n\}$ *be a sequence of n keys; and let* $C = \{c_1, c_2, ..., c_{m+n-1}, c_{m+n}\}$ *be the merge of A and B. Then* c_1 *is either* a_1 *or* b_1 *and for all positive integers i, the pair* (c_{2i}, c_{2i+1}) *will contain either* a_j *or* b_j *for some even integer j and either* a_k *or* b_k *for some odd integer k.*

Proof Replace each key in A with the word ODD or EVEN depending on whether the key has an odd index or an even index. Similarly, replace each key in B with the word ODD or EVEN. So at the start we have:

A	ODD EVEN ODD EVEN ODD EVEN ODD EVEN ...
B	ODD EVEN ODD EVEN ODD EVEN ODD EVEN ...

The first key in C, $c_1 = \min(a_1, b_1)$, so it has an odd index (in A or B) and after it is moved from A or B into C, either the A sequence or the B sequence now starts with an even index and the other sequence still starts with an odd index so we have:

Key sent to C	Keys remaining in A and B
ODD	EVEN ODD EVEN ODD EVEN ODD EVEN ...
	ODD EVEN ODD EVEN ODD EVEN ODD EVEN ...

Note that we left off the labels A and B because it doesn't matter which of them starts with an odd index and which starts with an even index.

Now we consider what happens when c_2 and c_3 are moved from the A and/or B sequences into C. There are three cases:

Case 1 Both c_2 and c_3 come from the sequence headed by a key with an even index.

Keys sent to C	Keys remaining in A and B
EVEN ODD	EVEN ODD EVEN ODD ...
	ODD EVEN ODD EVEN ODD EVEN ...

Case 2 Both c_2 and c_3 come from the sequence headed by a key with an odd index.

Keys sent to C	Keys remaining in A and B
	EVEN ODD EVEN ODD EVEN ODD ...
ODD EVEN	ODD EVEN ODD EVEN ...

Case 3 Key c_2 comes from one sequence and c_3 comes from the other sequence.

Keys sent to C	Keys remaining in A and B
EVEN	ODD EVEN ODD EVEN ODD ...
ODD	EVEN ODD EVEN ODD EVEN ...

Note that in all three cases, sequence C receives an even-indexed key and an odd-indexed key and one of the A and B sequences starts with an even index and the other starts with an odd index.

Note that the state of the A and B sequences after c_2 and c_3 are removed is the same as the state of these sequences before c_2 and c_3 are removed - one sequence starts with an even index and the other starts with an odd index. Thus, when we consider the removal of c_4 and c_5 we have the same three cases with the same results, etc. For all positive integers i, the pair (c_{2i}, c_{2i+1}) will contain either a_j or b_j for some even integer j and either a_k or b_k for some odd integer k so the theorem is proven. Note that the theorem is true whether sequences A and B are in ascending (non-decreasing) order or not.

Theorem 2.1 The Zero/One Principle *If a series of comparators sorts all 2^N sequences of N zeroes and ones then it will also sort any sequence of N arbitrary keys.*

Proof The 0/1-Principle can be proven by showing that if a series of comparators fails to sort some sequence of N arbitrary keys then there exists a sequence of N zeroes and ones that the series of comparators will also fail to sort.

Table I.1 The Proof of min(A, C) < min(B, D) [1]

$A < C$ and $B < D$	$A < C$ and $D < B$
• min(A, C) = A	• min(A,C) = A
• min(B, D) = B	• min (B,D) = D
• min(A, C) < min(B, D) → A < B	• min(A, C) < min(B, D) → A < D
• *Proof*	• *Proof*
Follows from the assumptions	A < C by min(A,C) and
	C < D by assumption
	It follows that A < D
$C < A$ and $B < D$	$C < A$ and $D < B$
• min(A, C) = C	• min(A, C) = C
• min(B, D) = B	• min(B, D) = D
• min(A, C) < min(B, D) → C < B	• min(A, C) < min(B, D) → C < D
• *Proof*	• *Proof*
C < A by min(A,C) and	Follows from the assumptions
A < B by assumption	
It follows that C < B	

Let S be a series of comparators and let $A = \{K[0], K[1], ..., K[N-1]\}$ be a sequence of N arbitrary keys that S fails to sort, i.e., when S receives A, it re-arranges A into some sequence $A' = \{K'[0], K'[1], ..., K'[N-1]\}$ with at least one index, j, where $K'[j] > K'[j + 1]$.

Let f be the function from the set of arbitrary keys into the set $\{0, 1\}$ where $f(x) = 0$ if $x < K'[j]$ and $f(x) = 1$ if $x > K'[j]$. Note that f is an isotonic function: if $x < y$ then $f(x) < f(y)$.

Let B be the sequence of N zeroes and ones formed by replacing $K[i]$ in A by $f(K[i])$ for $i = 0, 1, ..., N-1$; i.e., $B = \{f(K[0]), f(K[1]), ..., f(K[N-1])\}$. Since f is isotonic then the output of S when it receives B as an input will be $f(A') = \{f(K'[0]), f(K'[1]), ..., f(K'[N-1])\}$. But, $f(K'[j]) = 1 > f(K'[j + 1]) = 0$ so B is a sequence of N zeroes and ones that S fails to sort.

Theorem 3.1 [1] *Let A, B, C, and D be any keys. If*:

• $A \leq B$, *and*
• $C \leq D$, *and*
• *A and C are compared to find min (A, C) and max(A, C), and*
• *B and D are compared to find min(B, D) and max(B, D)*;

then:

• $min(A, C) \leq min(B, D)$; *and*
• $min(A, C) \leq max(A, C)$; *and*
• $min(B, D) \leq max(B, D)$; *and*
• $max(A, C) \leq max(B, D)$.

proof See Tables I.1 and I.2.

Table I.2 The Proof of max(A, C) < max(B, D)

$A < C$ and $B < D$	$A < C$ and $D < B$

• max(A, C) = C
• max(B, D) = D
• max(A, C) < max(B, D) → $C < D$
• *Proof*
  Follows from the assumptions
	• max(A, C) = C
	• max(B, D) = B
	• max(A, C) < max(B, D) → $C < B$
	• *Proof*
	  $C < D$ by assumption and
	  $D < B$ by max(B, D)
	  It follows that $C < B$

$C < A$ and $B < D$	$C < A$ and $D < B$
• max(A, C) = A • max(B, D) = D • max(A, C) < max(B, D) → $A < D$ *Proof* $A < B$ by assumption and $B < D$ (max(B, D)) It follows that A < D	• max(A, C) = A • max(B,D) = B • max(A, C) < max(B, D) → $A < B$ *Proof* Follows from the assumptions

Theorem 4.1 *Let A and A′ be any two 0/1-cases with the same number of keys and let C(Lo, Hi) be a comparison between any two of the keys, Lo and Hi. If A $\underset{=}{\ll}$ A′ before the C(Lo, Hi) operation is applied to A and A′, then A $\underset{=}{\ll}$ A′ after the C(Lo, Hi) operation is applied to A and A′ [1].*

Proof Assuming that A $\underset{=}{\ll}$ A′, we show the possible values of x and y before comparing the keys at locations x and y in the first four columns. In the second four columns we show the values of the keys at the locations x and y after comparing them. Inspecting Table I.3 shows that A $\underset{=}{\ll}$ A′ still holds after comparing the two keys at locations x and y.

Table I.3 The Proof of Theorem 4.1 [1]

Before comparing x with y				After comparing x with y			
$A[x]$	$A[y]$	$A'[x]$	$A'[y]$	$A[x]$	$A[y]$	$A'[x]$	$A'[y]$
0	0	0	0	0	0	0	0
0	0	0	1	0	0	0	1
0	0	1	0	0	0	0	1
0	0	1	1	0	0	1	1
0	1	0	1	0	1	0	1
0	1	1	1	0	1	1	1
1	0	1	0	0	1	0	1
1	0	1	1	0	1	1	1
1	1	1	1	1	1	1	1

Reference

1. Al-Haj BS, Batcher KE (2009) Finding faster sorting networks using sortnet. VDM Publishing House Ltd, Germany

Index

S. W. Al-Haj Baddar and K. E. Batcher, *Designing Sorting Networks*,
DOI: 10.1007/978-1-4614-1851-1, © Springer Science+Business Media, LLC 2011